Bottle Babies

Beneath The Belfry

James Bailey

A humorous look at those folks you've met at church.

Order this book online at www.trafford.com/07-1503
or email orders@trafford.com

Most Trafford titles are also available at major online book retailers.

Note for Librarians: A cataloguing record for this book is available from Library and Archives Canada at www.collectionscanada.ca/amicus/index-e.html

ISBN: 978-1-4251-3776-2

We at Trafford believe that it is the responsibility of us all, as both individuals and corporations, to make choices that are environmentally and socially sound. You, in turn, are supporting this responsible conduct each time you purchase a Trafford book, or make use of our publishing services. To find out how you are helping, please visit www.trafford.com/responsiblepublishing.html

Our mission is to efficiently provide the world's finest, most comprehensive book publishing service, enabling every author to experience success. To find out how to publish your book, your way, and have it available worldwide, visit us online at www.trafford.com/10510

www.trafford.com

North America & international
toll-free: 1 888 232 4444 (USA & Canada)
phone: 250 383 6864 ♦ fax: 250 383 6804
email: info@trafford.com

The United Kingdom & Europe
phone: +44 (0)1865 722 113 ♦ local rate: 0845 230 9601
facsimile: +44 (0)1865 722 868 ♦ email: info.uk@trafford.com

10 9 8 7 6 5 4 3 2

ACKNOWLEDGMENTS

I want to acknowledge my wonderful wife Marsha who has rolled her eyes and shaken her head at most of these stories for some 35 years, her forbearance in these matters will certainly add stars in her crown.

Also to my brothers in Christ, colleagues, and classmates Bob Harrison, Karl Jones, Anthony Bryant, and Bob Utley who have encouraged me to write this book in hope we might keep some young preacher from needlessly spending sleepless nights over some of the antics of these folks, I love you guys and your hearts of service.

During the writing of this book no one lent more encouragement, nor pushed me more to write than my long time teacher and friend Claudine Cervenka.

I was honored by her family to be asked to preach her funeral January 19, 2007 in Coleman, Texas. While preaching for the church in Coleman I would send her rough drafts of each chapter, she in turn would read them, laugh, and share them with someone else. She would tell me that each person –no matter where they went to church – thought they knew who I was talking about thus convincing me that these "bottle babies" exist in every fellowship.

Claudine has her fingerprints all over this book. I can't think of anyone I would have trusted more for their honest reactions. Claudine and I have been friends since she did her student teaching in my seventh grade English class well over 40 years ago. She laughed when she read these words and her laughter rings in my ears until this very day.

WARNING:

If you find yourself
in this book….
You might want to think
about changing your
outlook.

CONTENTS

BEFORE WE START – READ THIS

"Church" is a wonderful institution that has brought hope and peace to literally millions of people since it's beginning some 2000 years ago. And, it is understood that "church" is a commitment of heart, more than a literal building, or designated location. When all those folks who have made a commitment to God come together to praise, and worship God, something really special happens. Fellowship breaks out, outsiders are influenced by the message of the gospel, and the singing of praise to our heavenly King.

Being one of those people who can say "I have literally been attending church since the first Sunday after my birth" I can say with no fear of contradiction that "church" is a "Hap'nin'" each Sunday when some of the best folks in the world come together. And it is small wonder that people who scarcely know anything about God, His Word, or the mechanics of worship are inspired and influenced by just being in the midst of "church". These effects are small wonder when you consider that some of the great heroes of faith –men and women, moms and dads, boys and girls, and grand parents – walk through the doors of the church building each Sunday morning. While they may not be able to tell you exactly how that fish swallowed Jonah, nor the correct spelling of Habakkuk, they follow the teaching of God's Word, and live their lives with heaven in view.

The preceding words describe 99.9% of all church members. And then there is that other .1% that are present, everyone knows them, they wouldn't miss a meeting time—but they aren't sure why. For them something else has captured their attention, diverted their focus, or somehow surpassed heaven and being heaven bound in importance. It's the temperature of the meeting house, or the color of the carpet or "something" that has taken away all of their heavenly direction.

Now to be sure they will tell you that their particular focal point has some spiritual connection, but honestly it's hard to see even from the good seats up front.

Are they "good folks"? Absolutely. Do they have a "clue" about what's really happening at church? Not really. So what shall we do with that .1% that seems to "hold things back", or "get things off track"? Well my suggestion is we love them, we try to understand them, and to keep from crying over the bedlam they create, let's quietly laugh at their various shenanigans.

Come to think about it, what would church be like without them –probably a lot more boring! So, here's a few words about that .1% you will, no doubt, meet at church.

1

When Crossing Jordan Just Ignore that Sucking Sound

It was one of those glorious mornings. The children of Israel were living out their fondest dream. Already God had taken them through the middle of the Red Sea, and drowned their enemies behind them. Now they had come all the way to the bank of the river separating them from promise land, and their great leader, Moses, was standing before them giving them directions on how to take the new land, and what to be wary of as they took possession of the land. Somebody had the zany idea that they should send some spies in first, to see just how hard all of this was going to be. 12 men were chosen, one from each tribe, and they had now been gone several days searching out the secrets of the land.

All at once the word came down that the spies were coming! And now those men were standing before them. The whole nation of Israel was gathered into a single tent, the rustling of feet and the hushed whispers of the crowd grew silent. And then one of the spies stood and began to tell how the new land was indeed a land that flowed with milk and honey....milk.

About then Kireth, one of the young mothers in the audience, remembered that she had not yet fed her infant son that evening, so with every eye concentrated on the man speaking, she quietly reached for the goatskin of milk she had brought for the baby's bottle.

By this time 10 of the spies had spoken – and each one had told how the land was a wonderful land but that there were giants in the land and that taking it would be too difficult, and now there were even hushed whispers about going back to Egypt and the brick ovens.

But now it was Caleb's turn to speak. The crowd was already restless, as Caleb walked up onto the rock so that everyone could see him. He had a different outlook on taking the country, and he was about to urge them to take the land by faith in God who had promised it to the people.

But in the hush of the moment little Callib, Kireth's son, began to eat in earnest, and his smacking and slurping could be heard all through the camp.

Caleb did urge the people. He did tell them about having faith – but the fact is his entire message was diminished because what caught everyone's attention was Callib – that "bottle baby" in the tabernacle.

If you read the Biblical text you know the story, how the 10 unfaithful spies swayed the audience, and because of it all Israel wandered in the wilderness for 40 years while an entire generation died off.

But what about that baby, Callib? What ever happened to his descendants?

After all, he was in the younger generation who survived the wilderness, and at the age of 40 he watched the nation actually cross Jordan with Joshua and Caleb at the lead. But what about that infant that "stole the moment" 40 years earlier?

Well, in case you haven't noticed, he became the head of a mighty tribe. And his tribe of whiners and complainers, those who would take the attention off of the goals of the people of God, have descendants that exist to this very day.

In every part of Christendom , every sect, denomination and church the lineage of Callib can be found.

No matter how lofty the goals of a given group of God believers, more times than not there are some of those "bottle-babies" beneath their belfry there to steal all of the forward motion toward the goal God has set.

It might be a wonderful out-reach program designed to reach the masses and win a multitude of hearts for the Master, but it is derailed by the incessant "sucking noises" of those who are afraid the new folks might not be exactly to their liking. Oh, to be sure they want to do outreach – but they just want to control who's "outreached" and who isn't.

Again it might be a building program of Solomnic proportions – but again Callib's heirs will whine about how the old little buildings was good enough for their parents, and surely it would cost far more than the God of heaven could ever afford (this tribe holds firmly to the "God on welfare" position) and then they intone with whimpers of how there is really no need for a new building, and if it were built, surely it would never be filled. And the slurping and smacking starts to crescendo until the voice of reason, faith and logic is drowned out.

However, never do the descendants of Callib go into a whining, murmuring, sucking frenzy as they do when any mention of "Change" is raised. You see sitting there with Kireth on their favorite rock, nestled under that familiar blanket it looks, from their perspective, that they are in their own world, and even better, they are the only one *in* that private world. They cannot imagine that somewhere in the larger community of believers there might be someone who would be better served if a change took place. And one does not even have to discuss a change in some biblical doctrine that might be studied more deeply to invoke frenzy of whining and slurping. It can be something as opinion driven as the time of service, the time slot occupied by the Lord's Supper, and if someone should dare to suggest that the water cooler should be moved from under the staircase – well, ear plugs would surely have to be passed out to the entire congregation.

No matter how pure and unquestionable the judgment on a matter, and no matter how respected the one who gives an opinion of such a judgment matter, the "bottle-baby" tribe (from this point referred to simply as BBs) will rise up in opposition to attempt to steal any joy or victory from the moment.

Like many early tribes, the offspring of Callib have distinctive traits that can be easily recognized by anyone who has an enlightened eye.

The most recognizable trait is the hard set jaw, the lack of any expression that might be the result of faith. And this look is brought on by the deeply believed, but unspoken, conviction that God is really a 4 foot 3 inch, bearded, 100 year old man that weighs 700 pounds and couldn't possibly be able to move fast enough to have any affect whatsoever on the matter at hand.

But the trained eye must not miss the hands clinched into fists that are always in their pockets. This is to better facilitate holding on to nine cents of the first dime they ever beat their sister out of at the age of 6. And this "fist in the pants" posture also enables them to quickly find that little smooth stone (no, not the one that David used on Goliath) the little stone that they use when they pass gas so they can save half the stink. (NOTHING is to be wasted, you understand).

Next this tribe can be picked out in a crowd by the glazed, uninterested semi-glow from their eyes. It's not that they don't care...it's just that they don't care. This eye glaze has come from years of trying to maintain the appearance of being awake in worship when, in fact, 90% of their brain functions had ceased. In one congregation the preacher changed into his "end of sermon" tone too early, and 52 BB's jumped to their feet singing "Power in the Blood" in unison. That look of intense apathy is honed and sharpened over the years by having to think of other things to keep from learning some new Biblical truth. It has worked on their minds.

Finally, a definitive identification can be made by the nimble fingers of Callib's progeny in the way they can fold a one dollar bill 97 different ways so it leaves the impression it might be a ten or a twenty. And if, one bright

Sunday someone should, in passing, question what that folded currency was, the ready retort comes back, "You can't really know, can you?"

Bottle Babies like to engorge their opinions and remembrance of how much they give. This sort of mental gymnastics allow them to feel little pain when they begin a sentence in a church business meeting with "You know, I give a lot of money to this church..." It is also handy for them to add to the years of their tenure depending solely on who is still alive that knows they have only been in that congregation for 3 years. They will intone, "Well, I remember when this church...", when in fact they don't have the reference to remember much about this church at all.

Male BB's do their damage from a seat in a business meeting when they can confuse and confound almost any good idea causing it to "go into committee" until Jesus comes again. Or, the males also can stop most forward motion from a strategically chosen chair at most "eatin' meetins."

A doubt, properly placed in the mind of Bro. Mayi Askmywife, can quickly spread like wildfire. Always these doubts must be prefaced with "Several people have said…," or "A lot of people in this church feel..." Truth be known, most BB Christians don't know many people and they haven't opened up enough to "feel" with any of them.

It is a measurable fact however, that the most dangerous of this tribe are often the females. For these women the place of attack can be ladies Bible class, or an out of town trip for some women's program. Late at night in a rented motel room, in their chenille bathrobes and green "goop" on their faces (to hide their true identity) the ladies discuss what they are learning and then turn to what is happening "back home." At this point the female BB begins to whimper about the "poor widow women,", or "those families that just don't have much money,", or "where in the world will such changes end?" By interpretation – from the original language – that means, "I'll see we don't do this because my husband would feel obligated to give and I want new carpet," or "nobody asked me my opinion on the placement of the pulpit plants, so I'll just submarine their idea, too." If the female BB happens to also be the reigning matriarch of the congregation, the whining and smacking can be heard for miles. (Oh yes, every church has a matriarch – yes, even yours!)

Both male and female, one might note, have rearview mirrors instead of eyes.

Every year they live, the years gone before become more glorious, and the chances of ever attaining such glory again become more remote. Oh yes, and anything – animal, vegetable, or mineral that is over 20 years old becomes sacred. If it could be proven that one of those little glass - single - serving- communion cups had once been used by Leota Letitnot, who was her cousin's, nephew's second wife's aunt on her granddaddy's side, she would lobby the church to be "one cuppers" and have the preacher refill that little cup for each and every one of their one thousand members! And whine until it happened!

One would assume that in the process of learning the Biblical text that these BBs would eventually attain some sort of mental and spiritual growth.

Well, they would...but they don't study the text. They know "Jesus wept," "the plan of salvation" and assorted passages in Romans, all the time being skeptical of anyone who thinks they should know any of the other 64 books.

However, this lack of real study does have one very positive facet for the BB ("bottle baby") – it means that they can freely inter-mix cultural stories, and "chimney corner scripture" into any discussion, and do so at will.

Remember, that it was the father, of their forefather, who stood on the bank of the Red sea. And with the dust from the bottom of the sea still on his sandals, who would later own a set of clothes that didn't wear out for 40 years; who had just seen God lead them with His cloud by day and fire by night; and who stood there looking over into Promise land and said in a whiny voice just loud enough to pierce the hearts of the entire nation of Israel, "Oh it might have been better to die in Egypt! You know, those leeks and onions sure were good, yum, yum. Hey, I always thought making bricks in the sun was sort of fun! Nothing like a good whip lashing to get you started in the morning."

Like Kireth's little son, modern BBs are extremely set into a pattern. And, like her son, when the time comes to begin to take on spiritual steak and potatoes, there is an immediate, and all consuming, outcry. "Why if I had wanted to study I'd have enrolled in Bible College." Or more piously, "I just don't believe you have to know Greek and Hebrew to know the Bible so I don't see any reason for going any deeper into it." And the revered clincher,

"Let's just look at that next verse, and next week we'll cover the next one".

Perhaps the inclination for BBs to want to have a certain number or types of songs in the worship has been overstated. But sing more than one song that is unfamiliar, or from a projection screen or a printed handout, and the falling walls of Jerico could not match the racket that will be raised. It isn't that BBs don't like new songs – it is that they are so "snugly warm and comfortable" with the old ones. And to their credit, your average BB would sooner tolerate a new song – even on a printed handout – before they can sit silently, knowing that the furniture in the building has been rearranged or that their Bible class has been moved to a different room. So what, if they've gained 30 new members, "if they can't get in... they can't get in!"

No group of Bible believers can stand for long if this tribe is allowed to have much influence, however nothing will enrage and amplify these folks more than NOT being paid much attention. Suddenly the whining, smacking, slurping, and moaning is done through "little tiny sound sets". They very well may be the same words, and the same weak logic, only now it is done louder!

Whimpers are replaced with threats to leave the congregation. All the time knowing, that it will never happen because they couldn't stand to hear eight verses of "Thank God I'm free" being sung by the congregation as they walked out. If all this goes unchecked, then these "deep concerns" of the BB's start to show up in thinly veiled statements during prayers, or introductions of visiting speakers, or when the minutes of business meetings are typed. "Tonight we have visiting with us a wonderful guest speaker. He preaches the gospel that we all know and remember from days gone by. You are in for some preachin' tonight like you haven't heard in recent history.

Yes sir, this brother doesn't believe in changin' anything from its original and traditional meanings."

Even BB song leaders get into the act – "This morning we are going to sing one of the old standards of the church, one that has nourished our hearts through many times of trouble". And e-v-er-ytime he'll sing "Sing and Be Happy" to the tempo of Rock of Ages, because he doesn't want anyone to think that church is a place to be happy.

Then there are those introductions and prayers, "Our heavenly Father who is changeless and has shown us you do not like change." And of course, the next generation of BB's is grown in a Bible class. Statements like "I know when Bro. Went-to-school-when-I-Didn't taught this passage he said something else, but I just hold to the old gospel, and you never heard old Bro. Dead-for-a-hundred-years say or write anything like that!"

And pretty soon you will have a fairly large group who will gravitate to that BB teacher because of the promise of not having to learn anything new, and for the joy of being suspicious of everyone, and every other teacher, in the congregation. What fun!

And may the Lord richly bless in this life, and give a gold crown in heaven, to the person, male or female, who would dare to leave that group of "mentoree BB's," and come over to those who look deeply into God's Word. To get those books about Jesus out of their library to read, and actually color one of 'em, will set in motion a new round of slurping and whining.

BBs are very observant about "things." They watch "things." And if you should move or replace one of those "things" they will call you to immediate account. A church for years had deep red heavy curtains in front of their baptistery. Those things reached from the ceiling (25 feet up) to the floor. Well, some of the deacons decided to get a member who did stained glass to make a huge glass mural that would fill that space behind the pulpit and above the baptistery, leaving just enough room to see who was about to "go under." So, one night, after the glass was built, several of the young men came the building and took down those enormous drapes and replaced it with the new and beautiful stained glass. The next morning was Sunday, and when the whole congregation had assembled, there was much talk...not about the new stained glass, but rather, "Now I just want to know what was done with those wonderful old drapes. You know, old Bro.& Sis. Just Wright Acheck gave those to the church – donated them all by themselves back in 1955! Now I want to KNOW where they are!" Well, suddenly nobody knew, or at least a convenient case of amnesia has set in. But for several weeks, the poor Bro. that did the announcements was handed a note, and glared at, until he read it, about locating those precious old drapes. They should not have worried. It was later reported that those drapes were doing the best work of their existence by blocking the west sun off of several hundred prize laying hens belonging to one of the members.

There are, of course, times when certain people should be excused. Lars Sampson was developing a case of Alzheimer's so when he sometimes began to whine, we thought nothing of it. What did disturb us was when, even with the illness, he made better sense than some of the healthy folks.

And when people go through loss and traumas of other kinds, we all know that they must be given some extra understanding. However, for a healthy, church-going, God-believer to develop the aggravating attitude of being a BB, is something that just must be addressed.

In the next pages you will read descriptions of BB's that can be found in almost any religious group or organization.

The hope here is that you will recognize them and thereby minimize the damage they do, and, in the process have a good laugh, or at least a knowing smile as you visualize the person you think I am writing about. Oh yes, if you aren't from the south, and you think that "Bottle Babies" is too strong a term, well read on. Actually, the term my mama used for little kids that never grew up emotionally, was "titty babies".

2

The Spineless Old Brothers "May I. Askmywife" and His brother, "Yougo Askmywife"

Each Sunday the "ol' Askmywife Brothers " make their way to church. One of the brothers, that would be May I., comes in with a look on his face and a drag in his gait, which is unmistakably the mark of a man who has never had an original thought in his life. His mama raised him to be quick to answer to the dominant female in his life, and therein lay the main attraction for his present mate.

It matters little if you ask this brother "where are the light switches for the fellowship hall?" or if you should ask about "the theological ramifications of only taking two ants on the ark", the response will be the same. There will be a drop in his countenance, eyes that look around much like an inmate in a Nazi concentration camp looking for a peanut butter sandwich, and the stammered reply that "he isn't sure, but he could find out if you would just let him ask his wife." This knee jerk response comes from years of living with his wife Georgia Attilla, who is from the original Hunn family until 22 years ago when she became mated with a Askmywife. No one knows exactly how all that happened. We just know that at the wedding she hissed under her breath "don't ya?" and he replied "I do, dear! (and then he whispered, "did I say that right?")

However, you have to hand it to ol' Mayi (people sort of run his first name and initial together). He has persevered for all these 22 years to become a part of the scene at church. He is led in each Sunday by his wife Georgia, where they will find "their pew" in the place that the lighting and the air conditioning is just right for his wife. If someone should come by and try to start a conversation, his lips will never move. They haven't had to in 22 years because Georgia will interrupt before he can utter a sound.

That woman has filled in every blank in his conversations forever. Mayi thought he had found a place to "be heard" when he was made a deacon in the church. Those meetings rarely allowed women to be present, so in those confines Mayi could speak his mind. A couple of times he actually formulated a plan of action and swayed the entire deaconship to go along. Of course,at the next meeting, he suddenly had changed his mind on most of the details. Mayi knew that such antics made him look like he couldn't be counted on, but then that was a small price to pay to preserve the "hum of smoothness" at home.

The entire church remembered the noted Sunday – I think it was 20 years back – when in Bible class the teacher dared to ask Mayi a direct question about the text of the morning. Well, having had the lesson in his hands for a week, Mayi had actually studied the lesson and knew the answer. When that question came, he turned quickly to the poof passage, and opened his mouth to speak – but too late – Georgia Attila popped right in with her answer, and added "I'm sure Mayi wasn't sure about it anyway." It was as if Mayi had allowed the eyedropper of passion in his soul to explode, as he turned to Georgia Attila and said, in a voice just under the level of a sonic boom, "Shut up, Georgia!" It was noted that for a moment or two it was as if time stood still. We are sure birds quit singing and not a baby dared to cry, as Georgia

Attila sat there glaring at Mayi with her little pill box hat spinning out of control on her head, drilling the hat pin into her skull. "WELL!" she huffed, and exited the classroom as quickly, and with as much gusto, as she could.

As the doors closed there was a long moment of silence. And then, some doing it audibly, and others in their heart of hearts, applause sprang forth!

Ol' Mayi had never felt so "in control." He felt masculine, and his ego had been richly stroked, that is, until he got to the car after worship, endured the coldest drive ever for July, and arrived at his own home now encased in several sheets of ice. The dog, "Roadmap," didn't even know what was happening, but he knew better than to go near Mayi. Georgia Attila made one of those huge Hollywood turns, launched her pill box hat in the direction of Mayi, and in a screech that would shatter glass at 500 yards, she bellowed, "I have never been so humiliated in my life! If I want you to have an opinion, I'll give you one!" And right there on that bright Lord's Day morn she performed the first "Opinion-ectomy" ever performed on an adult male without anesthetic, and it has lasted until this very day.

But be assured it is no better over at the home of Mayi's brother "Yougo Askmywife." Yougo has been more or less happily married to the former Matilda Smithnwesson for nearly 30 years. It is true that there was a shotgun at their wedding, but not as you might think. That shotgun was there as insurance against Yougo backing out and her daddy having to take her back!

Yougo is confident. To see him, he makes a striking picture. Every other man in the church knows that Yougo is a "man's man". He wears the best suits, imported shoes and ties. He is immaculate. When he is asked to take a leading role in worship he does so with much gusto and aplomb. Did I say that every man sees Yougo that way? Well, not every woman. Matilda was a "high caliber" daughter of the influential Smithnwesson family. And when everybody was "oohing and ahhing" over some remark that Yougo had made, she would wait until they got home and explode "Yougo! You don't have half a brain! Now you may think that you are the head of this house but brother, I'm the neck! And don't you forget it!" Finally, Yougo got the message and when asked about much of anything, he would simply shrug and in one continuous tone say "you go ask my wife yourself, if you want to know", and turn and walk away. It is rumored that once he tried to act on his own conviction – something about buying a new car – but no one has ever seen the car, you see, she has never allowed him to back it from the garage. His only saving grace is that now he doesn't even try to answer questions himself, he just refers you to a "higher power", his wife. To cover his lack of "pluck" he is always ready with a sharp comeback, or a remark that would make metal weep. He also makes grand use of the "consistent loss of short term memory" which has gotten him out of many a sticky situation. His personal "motto" is "Oh, I don't remember saying that."

Once Yougo was asked to serve on the church board for a term. His commanding presence and ready quips added much to the otherwise mundane meetings. Since he owned his very own pocket calculator with his initials engraved on it, he was always helpful when it came to financial matters.

In a voice that resonated throughout the board room, he would announce how "at this rate the church will go bankrupt in no time flat." However, when matters of a spiritual nature would come up, Yougo would just slide down slightly in his chair and mutter something about needing to think it over for a day or two.

That is modern "chickenese" for "you boys just haven't heard my wife's side of it yet". That interpretation has never been clearer than the time that a local seminary received from Matilda and Yougo a sum of money to complete a building on campus. They asked the couple if they could put their name on the new structure. The school was trying to be nice, and the lettering would have looked really good, except that the original words "Yougo and Matilda Askmywife Conservatory of Opinionated Thinking" had been changed several times to read "Matilda and Yougo...Askmywife..Conservatory..." and then back to the original, and then...well you understand. Those letters have not yet been put on the building.

It has been said more than once, with tongue in cheek, that the congregation hopes that "she dies first"; if not, ol' Yougo may live forever waiting for Matilda's permission to go the Great Beyond.

Now understand, if you just looked at either of these brothers, you would not think of them as BB's. Both Askmywife brothers put forth a striking image. But they have never quite weaned themselves from the milk of allowing someone else to keep them from taking a stand. And the church is gagging on their lack of growth. When you see these two BB's you just have to smile, or maybe laugh. If you don't, you'll cry.

3

Ruby Beth Honnibunch – Matriarch

Ruby Beth, or "Ms. RB" as she is referred to by the wise of the congregation, is the daughter of Bro. Herman Slackinthebritches and his wife Corra. Ruby Beth has been "at" church or "in" church almost all of her life. As a child she developed her talents by consistently causing her teachers to cry by asking questions that a seminary professor could not answer. And then upon entering High School and puberty, at about the same time, she began to litter her path with the tears and whines of various young men who were determined, as they say, to "break this filly to a walk". Didn't happen. In fact, as the years aged Ruby Beth and gave her character, her resolve to be the "force to be dealt with" increased to biblical proportions.

You may wonder how RB ever got to be the matriarch of her congregation. Well, it was the outcome of a period of time the church refers to as "The Great Wars". Just prior to this period of time the reigning matriarch, Sally Ann Sourkisser, had unrepentantly died without anointing her successor.

That created a situation much like a "jump ball" in a basketball game.

Every well bodied, influence-seeking female in the church went into high gear. Nobody was sure if the church would first be stamped out by covered dishes or sweet letters of appreciation. I mean, even ol' Bro. Drupe, who hadn't been at church in 20 years and couldn't care less, got 20 letters of appreciation for his support. Each Sunday the duel would bring a foyer table full of pretty sacks with "just a little something" in them, for some other woman whom they barely knew. And speaking of "teas", we had 'em. Every night, at noon, and Sunday afternoon there would be a "tea" for just about every imaginable reason. Now you must understand that a "church tea" is the ecclesiastical equivalent to a televised presidential speech. It provides the giver of the "tea" to expound her opinions on every "stupid decision" the men of the congregation have ever made. Now, don't misunderstand, there is an ample amount of "Bless his heart" and "poor thing" thrown in to make it all seem on the highest order. And then the momentum of the "teas" would carry over into the fellowship time before and after Sunday worship, when the terms "precious" and "darling" were just about worn from the English language. Oh yes, and these women who were vying for the top influence and power-wielding spot in the congregation used the word "fun" to the point of nausea for anyone who was listening. "Fun?" Not one of those ol' girls had had any fun in their lives, until this competition began. Now they tossed around statements like "Yes, I think new artificial shrubs for the pulpit would be *fun* to do", and "Painting the back hallway that leads to the baptistery Hellfire Red would be a fun thing to do."

Understand, when the smoke clears in a week or two (Unless we have two really obstinate competitors) a smile will never be seen on the face of the winner again, and the word "fun" will be stricken from her vocabulary, and by rule, from the life of her poor husband. (Somewhere it is written that a widow is really better suited for the role of Matriarch because she doesn't have to punish some unwitting male in the process.) When Sister Sourkisser was matriarch, people would stop and shake their heads and pray for Sylvester, her husband, who walked meekly two steps behind her at all times, and often would be summoned to her side by a sharp whistle and sucking noise from her pursed lips. And everyone would say, or at least think, "that's Sylvester Sourkisser... bless his heart."

What had gone on behind the scenes during the times of the Great Wars was that each combatant for matriarch had put her mate into basic training so that he would be all "shaped up" if the office fell to his wife. Suddenly the poor men found themselves not being able to laugh in church, even at a sermon joke. They could not smile, even at the most humorous moment, and if either of these rules were broken, the ice in the stare they were given, would have easily chilled the margaritas he needed to survive. At home, at just the right moment in his favorite TV program, the "candidate for matriarch" would break in with a scathing denunciation of whatever the poor man had done that day. It didn't matter what, this was just "practice". And to the poor husband, it was like going to spring training for the death chamber.

Ruby Beth Honnibunch "won" the entire competition "flat out" when she successfully opposed a move in the congregation to have designated parking spaces for visitors. RB didn't really care either way, she and her spouse always parked in the handicapped space at the back anyway. (She said being married to "Har-r-ry" was handicap enough.) But the main object in it all was to derail some well thought of program of the male members to prove that she was "a force to be reckoned with". Statements were couched in sweetness that would force your blood sugar to new medical heights.

"Why we have never had such designated spaces before, because our facility was so well designed in the first place. I just believe that the warmth of our church is such a reward that any visitor would be glad to park in the next county once he gets inside our building. You know, my old papa had a bad leg and used to let my mother out at the door and park in another zip code and still make it in before the end of the first hymn. Really now, I don't see the need to make all these extravagant changes." Well, it worked! Not only did she cut down the number of visitors at church (known by Ruby Beth as "those who don't know the rules around here"), but she dumbfounded the men, and left all the other candidates with nothing to do for a rejoinder.

Let it be known that Matriarch is not an office that is officially recognized nor sanctioned by the church. There were no coronation parades, there were no official titles pronounced, nor diamond tiaras handed out. You will not find the name of the winner of the Great Wars written down in any set of business meeting minutes of the church, but let there be no doubt that the next Sunday morning after the killing of the visitors parking spaces, when Ruby Beth Honnibunch and her husband Har-r-y came in to worship, even the birds stopped singing. Little out-of-control children ran to their mothers and stood there barely breathing, and every head turned and nodded and acknowledged the transfer of power that had taken place in the female pecking order of the church. Ruby Beth was 45 when she took office. That isn't necessarily good. You see the average life span of the matriarch is 90 years.

One might think that all that pent up-tension, and never smiling outlook on life might cause the life expectancy of the matriarch to be shorter. Not at all. We all know that God is in charge of the days of our lives, and even God is careful in messin' with a "shore 'nough" matriarch of a local church.

If all of this seems like a terrible thing, let me assure you that it can be worse.

One congregation has had a Great grandmother, grandmother, mother and daughter who were all matriarch in succession. When that last generation got old enough to take her turn, she entered the position with the most benevolent of acts – she fired the church leadership, stole the church bank account, and dissolved the charter of the church. She and her husband, Benoit, took the money and moved to Montana where she lives today as a District Court judge. Did all that upset the church? Naw, they just sang "Free At Last" as the doors closed and the Pizza equipment was moved in.

4

Brother "Cleve" Who's Gonna Leave

No one ever suspected when Bro. Cleveland Thinskin and his wife Taloola moved to the congregation that these seemingly nice people would turn out to be such Bottle Babies. When "Bro. Cleve" first arrived, he made it plain that he wanted to be involved. And he and Taloola went to every fellowship meal armed with her "killer baked beans" which were about the consistency of 50 weight motor oil. The Thinskins quickly picked up on every tradition of fellowship meetings in their new church home. "Cleve" even took his turn at teaching Bible class. And, to say the least, he did bring some variety to the educational department. There he stood with his green plaid suit, two-tone shoes, neck tie that was wide enough to catch and stop those baked beans in their tracks. He had a yellow note pad that had notes on every page, and he would periodically flip back and forth from front to back as if searching for some profound, but missing, point he wanted to make. That suit was , as I was informed, "a doozy". And that description is pretty accurate since there was so little natural material in that thing that most dogs and sheep would ignore it all together. It did sadden one to think of how many little "polyesters" had to give their lives for that suit.

Our first hint about the real nature of ol' "Cleve" should have come when we noticed he started each and every class with "Now I've been a member of the church for a number of years..." and then he would take off his glasses and put one ear piece in his mouth, which pretty much gagged the class since we had all seen those glasses up close. Then "Cleve" would launch off into some homespun philosophy about some point that two pole vaulters with a helicopter couldn't have connected to the subject from the text. Text – that brings me to that copy of the Bible "Cleve" always carried. "Big as a horse's leg!" It was quickly agreed that he would never be allowed to teach in the children's class because if he dropped that Bible on one of those kids it would surely take his or her life.

As I said, the church was enjoying the variation from the normal sight in Bible class, when someone suggested that maybe "Cleve" should stay a little closer to the subject as it was laid out in scripture. At first there was a long pause of complete silence, as everyone quit breathing. Then "Bro Cleve" fairly exploded. He put his glasses back on and stared over the top rim right at the offending person. His eyes squinted into two little slits, and his voice took on the tone of a 747 taking off. He said "Well, I'll just tell you what! If this church isn't willing to sit still for some plain Bible teaching and avail itself of my years of Bible study, then I'll just make it easy on you and just leave." And with that, he motioned to Taloola and they left!

Now, when I said that "He motioned for Taloola" that wasn't as fast as it sounded. You see, Taloola was sitting near the back trying her best to chew her bubble gum while doing her fingernails. And "Cleve's" sudden command to vacate her pew upset her new polish job. She spilt that "Passion of the Heart Red" nail polish all over her electric blue dress. And that dress was tight enough so there was nothing to stop the red liquid until it ran off the material and onto her electric blue four-inch – stiletto pumps.

We had heard Taloola speak about "what a spiritual man Cleve' was at home". And for a while we didn't doubt a word she said. Then the thought crossed a few observant minds, "If he is so spiritual, what is he doing with her?" The woman, I was told by the ladies Bible class chairperson, had "Hussy" written all over her.

Anyway, for the next several months, member after member, the preacher, several deacons, and a widow or two would try to speak to "Cleve" at the store or somewhere else in town, and try to talk him into coming back to church. However, all their efforts were in vain. After a while it became evident that all this attention and pleading affected "Cleve" and Taloola like a duck at a June bug festival. They were loving it. "Cleve" would wrinkle his brow and look pious while Taloola would chew her gum furiously and look at the ground, as person after person tried to pursued them. Then Taloola would just look at "Cleve" with eyes full of understanding and say "Baby, that church just isn't worthy of your talent!" And with that, the interview was over.

A visiting preacher came in one Sunday and the topic of "Cleve" and Taloola came up. He asked, "How long did they stay here? And what did he get mad about this time?" After having it all explained, the visiting preacher said, "Well, over where I preach, they only stayed two weeks and got mad because we didn't serve imported coffee during Sunday School. We're pretty sure we hold the record for "Shortest Stay by the Thinskins". Over a period of several years, "Cleve" and Taloola Thinskin placed their membership at every congregation of the church in a 500 mile radius of their home. One day we got a call that "Cleve" had passed away. And a few felt that they should attend the funeral. I think it was because they felt that in some way we were responsible for him leaving our church. If, in fact, there was a drop of deep sentiment left, it evaporated like an ice cube on a black '55 Buick when they got to the cemetery and saw the inscription on the headstone. It read, "Here lies Cleveland Thinskin

Loving Husband of Taloola and
Faithful member and Bible Teacher
Having taught the truth across the land". Uh-huh. And Amen.

5

Bro. Argus is "Agin' It"

By now, some who read this book may think that the author is just "makin' fun" of different personalities in the church. That I think they are worthy of being made fun of – and that I must be "possessed" to see something funny in these matters. We-l-l-l. that's right. And I consider it one of the finest gifts ever bestowed on mortal man by the Almighty. Fact is, unless we laugh about these folks, the weeping and wailing over the future of the church will be heard internationally.

And that brings me to "Bro. Argus Spectator", and his loyal wife of 52 years Audeen. The Spectators were always present at every meeting. It didn't matter if it was for worship, or Bible Class, or a pot-luck dinner, they were there. The only troublesome point with these Bottle Babies was that no matter where they were, there was always something going on that Bro. Argus was "agin'".

While it was true, that Argus had been around that congregation for as long as anyone could remember, Argus infuriated most everyone when he would begin each denunciation with "I've been a member here all my life, and I tell you I'm agin' that!" First, it was rearranging the furniture in the sanctuary. Then, he was "agin'" those new Baptism garments with their "outrageous" color. (Royal blue as I remember). Interesting thing, if his "agin statements" didn't get enough notice he would think up some plausible reason to go with them. Once the ladies changed the floral arrangements in the main sanctuary (first time they had been changed since 1972) and Bro. Argus was "agin it". When asked why, he told them that "those flowers made his allergies act up."

That's when someone informed him that they were artificial! You would have thought that such a rejoinder would have caused him embarrassment, but not "Bro. Argus." He simply switched to another point, and informed everyone that the colors chosen were "ga-aw-w-dy!" And with that, stormed out of the building.

Bro. Argus' favorite ploy though was to attack every new program or project with the same aggrandizing lead sentence – "You know, I give a lot of money to this church...". Well, the fact was that we didn't know. It is one of those unspoken rules in the church that no one should pay attention who gives what, or how much. Like the Bible says "Don't let the left hand know what the right hand is doing," you know. So not one person who heard Argus' pronouncement had the slightest idea how much he gave, if anything. And no one could deny that the weight of such logic would fairly choke the life out of and new undertaking by simply speaking those words. With that ploy, Argus successfully defeated buying new trees for the yard, fresh paving for the parking lot and buying better quality toilet paper for the women's restroom. (Something about "splinters"....I don't know.) Argus used that same statement to bury plans for a new bus, handicapped parking spaces, and a new sign for the front of the building. New water fountains, changing tables in the nursery, and new tables for the fellowship hall were all crushed by Argus. Each summer Argus and Audeen would take a two week vacation. The church referred to those two weeks each year as "freedom Sundays".

This maneuver of Argus' went on until a minister that had served at the congregation several years before came back to preach a revival. The preacher knew all the men of the congregation , and he knew Argus Spectator. The memory was fresh on his mind of how Bro. Argus had single-handedly defeated a plan to move the church to the most prestigious piece of property in the county and to build a new sanctuary there to the glory of God. Besides, in the two days he had been back, he had received not less than 20 phone calls from members asking him to "please do something about Argus so this church can "move forward". The preacher was brought to mind of one of his favorite Bible stories, about the children of Israel being made to wandered in the wilderness for 40 years before they were allowed to go to Promiseland. The preacher had often wondered what that last Israelite from the older generation must have felt like when every morning he was awakened by people peering under his tent to see if he was "still" alive. And then as the oldest male of that faithless generation stepped from his tent into the morning sunlight, he was greeted by an orchestra of groans from the rest of the 3 million Israelites, for they knew they would have to wander one more day. Imagine, he thought, what it would be like to have everybody know that "if you would just pass on, we could go to Promiseland".

Well, in the mid-week business meeting that week, the visiting preacher was present by invitation. And sure enough someone brought up replacing the dishwasher in the fellowship hall that had been broken since Johnson was President. Bro. Argus spoke up and said, "I just want you to know that I give a lot of money to this church...", and before he could finish the sentence, the visiting preacher said "How much?" Argus was dumbfounded that anyone would dare ask such a question. "Well, it is a substantial amount, I'll have you to know. And you would sure miss it if it stopped!" exploded Argus.

The preacher hardly looked up from the hymnal he was holding, "How much do you give to this church? You are always talking about it, you are obviously proud of the amount, so HOW MUCH?!" Ol' Bro. Argus got this pious look on his face, dropped his eyes and said sanctimoniously, "Bro. I don't believe that is any of your business, nor the business of any other person here. You know the Bible says "Let not the right hand know...", but the preacher interrupted his thought. "I know perfectly well what that verse says, but I still want to know "HOW MUCH?" Argus asked, in a voice that was obviously shaken, "Why do you think I should tell you? That's really between God and me. So, why is it so important that I tell you how much I give?"

The preacher arose from his chair, went to face "Bro. Argus" and pointed his finger in his face as he said "Because when you tell us, we're going to take up a collection and BUY YOU OUT!" The whimpering and whining and sucking noises on that night would have drowned out the whimpering in the eternal depths, when a soul is snatched from Hell's fire. "Bro. Argus" collapsed in his chair, and his face turned the color of someone somewhere between faint and dead.

At the end of the meeting, when Argus didn't move from his chair, Audeen was called to come drive "Argus" home. When she laid eyes on her husband she started a sort of "mantra" as she left, "he's a good man, you know he's been here a long time, I hope you don't think too badly of him.....come on baby, Mama is going to make it alright." And with that, they left.

It was reported that the next night at the revival, Argus wasn't there, but Audeen was, and she fairly "jumped in the middle" of that preacher for what he had done to Argus. The preacher just repeated the question to Audeen, and she too left peaceably, though ruffled. Seizing the opportunity, the church asked a member, who was also president of the local bank, for a $100,000 loan which was granted. And they scoured the minutes of the business meetings so they could put into place every project that had been suggested and killed by Argus.

Audeen still lives in the community and still comes to church. And each new member must spend some time hearing about how that preacher declawed "Bro.Argus."

It is sort of a mystery, how folks who are just always "Agin' things", and would never think of teaching a class, keeping the nursery, or serving on any committee that would make the church grow, should exert any pressure upon, or have the ear of, the church.. no matter how much money they contribute.

After all, that money was God's before it was theirs, and what God is interested in are those folks that "DO" with the money that is available.

This sort of BB has developed no appreciation for the ongoing nature of the church and has never thought about the good intentions nor the wise thinking of others in the church. Their entire goal in life is to "keep things like they have always been", no matter how bad that might be.

6

Percival the Penny-Pincher

Percival Primrose and his wife Penny had been members of the local congregation for as long as anyone could remember. Penny (daughter of S.D. and Maxine Scrounger) had grown up in that church . And no one could forget the "happy day" when Penny Scrounger became Penny Primrose. Most agreed it was a shame that she couldn't have changed her name while she was still dating. Anyway, Percival was a good-enough man, with his very pointed hat, pointed shoes, and the sharpest pointed nose you have ever seen!

That nose, accented by the black "Ricky-Racoon" glasses, and his always buttoned, three button suit of gray plaid, presented a sight that would make most forward thinking church members fall over in a dead faint.

The story goes that as an infant his mother dropped a roll of dimes into his crib accidentally, and scared the little tike to death, and Percival has been holding on to his pennies ever since.

Each month the church secretary dutifully prints out her monthly financial report. There are always 250 fresh clean copies on the foyer table for anyone who cares to pick it up. Most months 249 of them stay right on that table until they are retrieved and thrown away when the next edition comes out. However, that ONE copy is "gone over" with a fine-tooth comb by Percival Primrose. Percival considers it a cardinal infraction if the decimal points don't all line up on the page. One can only imagine how he reacted when the church bought several cases of memo paper that could have been purchased for $.41 less at a store in a city 100 miles to the south. Percival made it a point to expound on the fact that such savings, over time, would have amounted to "monumental money" in the long run. Once someone suggested that a new sanctuary could be built for something over $750,000 and they had to take Percival to the hospital and put him under oxygen.

And don't think all of this "frugality to the fifth power" was only practiced by Percival. No-o-o sir! Mrs. Penny Primrose was no "slouch" either. At her home she placed bricks in the toilet tanks to save water, put a timer on the shower to make Percival hurry when he took a bath, and it was rumored that she had a match box taped under her sewing table labeled, "String too short to use".

Penny Primrose always remembered the words of her dear mother Maxine when she said, "If you can throw it away, you probably shouldn't". Penny never did know exactly what that meant, but she always remembered it. So now she subscribed to every "cost-cutting" "Penny-saving" magazine and book club in the country. When the floral centerpiece for the ladies class had seen its 23rd year, someone suggested that it should be replaced. That remark caused Mrs. Penny to rise from her chair and launch into a series of reasons why money for a new arrangement was just a WASTE! In fact, the series of "How to restore your cheap artificial and plastic plants" went on for several Sunday afternoons, with a grand attendance, since no one wanted to be labeled a "spendthrift" – especially by Sister Primrose.

Meanwhile Percival had discovered "recycling". And with Percival it wasn't a matter of saving the trees, or keeping the landfills from overflowing, it was the very thought of "Not having to buy something new, when something could be used over again" that really got his attention. A member of the congregation, who was also an insurance man, one day gave Percival a brand new note pad, one of his advertising trinkets. Well, ol' Percy' just thanked him over and over and repeatedly. You see he had stayed in several feet of hot water with Mrs. Penny because he refused to use a clean sheet of paper to make a list of things she needed from the store. Well, after about the 49th list being made on the same piece of paper there was no telling what the poor man was going to come home with from the store. Percival even got so "bumfuzzled" one night he called home asking Penny where in the world he was supposed to find deodorant eggs and Leggs pantiliners. Well, the gift of the new note pad was going to stop all that abuse. However, someone did discover in Percival's car, a small box containing every piece of paper he had ever used, so that he could reuse them at a later date. Ms. Penny was not impressed.

It wasn't that the Primroses were poor folks, neither did they lack for anything they really wanted. It was a personality quirk. The best explanation was voiced in a men's business meeting one afternoon after Percival had suggest recycling the water in the baptistery. Onc anonymous person suggested that perhaps it was by being "tight" that Percival forced enough blood to his head to stay conscious. It was thought that if he relaxed and operated by faith, be might just die for lack of enough stress to keep his blood flowing.

Percival's real problem was that he didn't understand that the church runs on a "faith economy" – Percival was sure it ran on garage sales and recycling drives, and watching every cent spent so closely that the likelihood of anything actually being spent was remote, to say the least. And the result of the onslaught of "tightwadiness" was predictably chilling. No one wanted to use a charge card or credit account for fear of having to give the receipts to Percival who was now the new treasurer for the church. (Someone with a real sense of humor thought they might as well "use his talent") The kindergarten class was learning to melt the old Crayolas together to make exciting "new colors", and the teen-age girls were learning how to make pillow corsages out of used Kleenex. Percival could often be seen in the office erasing the writing on response cards so they could be used again, and he insisted that if you were baptized you HAD to take your baptismal robe and towel home and launder it yourself. Now, if it is true that you should always find something good to say about a person, well let me tell you, dear reader, ol' Percival had a curious talent, the likes of which have never been seen before. Percival could follow the deacons down the aisle as they took up the contribution, and just from the sound he could calculate the "take" within 15 cents of the bank statement.

Finally the stress took its toll and Percival died. Penny honored his wishes and had him "laid away" in two computer boxes, from the alley behind the local hardware store, duct taped together. The last thing anyone ever saw of Percival as those six strong men carried him from the church were the words written on the end of one of those boxes....something we never connected to Percival in this life ...there it was , the words, "USER FRIENDLY".

7

Whomovia Wannamaker – i.e. "Ms. Anonymous"

For many years no one was sure whom "Ms. Anonymous" actually was. But that isn't to say that she didn't make her presence felt at every inopportune moment. When the ladies' class wanted to change the day of their meetings there was that "letter" stating how it was a part of the historical past of this church that the Ladies Class always met on Monday, and there would surely be full scale fall-out in the congregation if this tradition was breached" – signed Ms. Anonymous.

And when a call was made for new board members, not a soul said a word about any of the nominees, except "Ms. Anonymous" who wrote scathing letters about all but one of the candidates, stating everything from their political preference to their love life as reasons why they should not be considered. The congregation wondered about that "one man" that wasn't "written up," and for a time the smart money thought that Ms. Anonymous had to be the wife of Silas Weed, the local feed store operator. But Sally Weed denied it with such verve that the notion was finally dropped.

Nevertheless the letters just kept on coming. There was one against rearranging the furniture in the sanctuary; another about the noisy children and how their parents ought to take them to the nursery, and teach them to behave in church. Still another epistle of negativity came as the plans were being drawn up to purchase the lot beside the church building and build a play ground for the children of the church. That letter stated that although she understood that parents of little children needed a safe place to play after Bible school and after worship services, she just couldn't understand why this generation of children couldn't play in the street "where so many other children have played before." The letter went on to state that any church that couldn't afford to fix up the needed repairs to the homes of its widows, just wasn't in any situation to be buying "recreational space for the kids."

No one was immune from the poisonous pen of this clandestine woman. She wrote to the preacher and scolded him for not visiting more and especially those who were in the hospital, and also mentioned that he really DID need to spend more time at home with his own children. Then Ms. Anonymous wrote to the church secretary to inform her that the least she could do would be keep up with who was actually "in" the hospital and those who were already at home. She was particularly incensed with the fact that our secretary couldn't seem to make the bulletin look better, and particularly easier to read. However, I suppose the zenith of her letter writing came when she verbally mounted the youth minister for his choice of clothes. Why, she had seen him just the other day wearing a T-shirt, his swim trunks, and a towel tied around his waist. Didn't he know that a "man of the cloth" – even if it was a "Jr. Man of the Cloth" – should always wear clothes befitting his position?

The youth minister would have loved to explain that he was on his way to the local YMCA for a swim at the time, but how could he, the letter was signed "Ms. Anonymous." And therein lay the power, and the devilishness, behind all of her letters – no one could defend themselves against her attacks.

I suppose we would have gone on forever not knowing *who* "Ms. Anonymous" was except that after one Sunday night meeting a "discussion" broke out in the foyer (actually it was a full blown brouhaha, complete with yelling, crying, and words that most Would War I vets have yet to hear.)

In the middle of it was one of the local church leaders, and Mrs. Whomovia Wannamaker. Whomovia, named by her paternal grandmother, was a slight little lady with a "librarian bun" hairdo. Standing only four feet nine inches tall and tipping the scales at a whopping 89 pounds, she was very easy to overlook. Anyway, that night the music director had led the congregation in several songs, none of which Whomovia had ever sang before. They were too fast for her to "sight read", and the words were so unfamiliar that she couldn't read them fast enough through her "milk bottle bottom" glasses, so she just didn't get to join in. Well, Whomovia was mulling around the foyer after worship quietly moaning and groaning to anyone who would listen about how she "just didn't get anything out of the music that night". After several moments of not getting the results she wanted, she approached one of the church leaders and, with appropriate whine in her voice, she voiced her complaint. The leader, who was in a big hurry to get home to his favorite TV show "Touched by a Millionaire", simply said – with no malice intended – "Well, we just don't get it our way everytime", and turned to go. Well, that sort of "depressed the handle in ol' Whomovia's churn" – and she exploded with various and sundry opinions as to WHY that "lame brained excuse for a music leader ought to be drawn and quartered on the spot". But the part that got everyone's attention was the statement when she said "You people just don't listen to us church members! Why I have written letter after letter........". The proverbial cat, had just gotten out of the proverbial bag and hit the proverbial fan. Suddenly a dozen people's ears picked up, and they began to ask Whomovia about this letter and that, in such a way that she had to either lie about it, or admit she had written them. She was far too "holy a lady" to ever lie, so she admitted to them all. The result of that confrontation was that there hasn't been a decent anonymous letter written in that congregation for three years now. There is more confidence and more peace among the workers without the threat of such letters. And oh yes, the church leader was given an "Outstanding Service Award" at the very next luncheon. Now, on the rare occasion something is received that isn't signed, you can drive by Whomovia's house and there is a little placard in the window that reads "'Twern't ME!"

8

Seth and Smitti Sacredrocks, collectors of anything ever used at church

Rumor has it that Seth and his wife Smitti came to the local congregation when asked to move from their former home by the local sanitation department. Not that they were not clean and well kept, it was just that their three bedroom house with a double car garage was completely full of at least "six bedrooms" of assorted "stuff" they had rescued from their last place of worship.

It seemed that every time the local church was having a work day, when all the closets, storerooms and classroom lecterns were going to be cleaned out, that Seth and Smitti would station themselves at the entrances to the buildings so they could inspect every parcel of refuge taken from those sacred premises. As fast as some well intentioned fellow member could carry out some worn out Sunday school quarterlies, Smitti would haul them back in muttering under her breath about how some folks just don't have a sense of sacred history. The marriage of these two must have been made in heaven, but if that is true, it was the only wedding ever performed in heaven with a borrowed wedding dress, plastic flowers from several family funerals, and a wedding cake on loan from the local deli. Anyway, Seth, a man recently retired as a local grain buyer, would bring his talent for dealing in hundredths of a cent, to every discussion about replacing any of the furnishings of the church building. Once the men of the congregation decided that the youth minister should have a proper desk, since the one he was using was really two, two drawer file cabinets with an old door laid across them. Not to incur too much wrath from Seth, the men had gone to a second-hand office furniture store and purchased a desk recently removed from a bank. As the old door and scarred up cheap filing cabinets were wheeled from the building, Seth was heard to question. "Now what do you think is so wrong with THEM? After all they have served well for some of the best youth men in the business, and there is no telling the stories that desk could tell about the kids that have been counseled around it." One of the men laughingly suggested if it was so special they would be glad to take to take it to Seth's house, and to everyone's amazement, he accepted! "Amazed" probably isn't the right word. You have to understand that for years, after a "good housecleaning" had taken place, late in the dead of night, after all the houses were dark, and the local police were on break down at the Wide Awake Cafe, those bags of debris taken from the buildings would mysteriously disappear. The locals all thought, for a long time, that it was the local sanitation department making early rounds at the church dumpster, but one night one of the church leaders couldn't sleep so he was driving by the building and noticed that the bags of trash put out just a few hours before, were missing. The whole affair was quite a "who-done-it" among the congregation for several years, until Seth and Smitti had a garage sale at their house. While people were milling through two tables piled high with nothing worth more than a dime, someone stepped around behind the shed at the Sacredrocks, and there was every scrap and piece of debris and trash ever removed from the local church. There were old hymnbooks so worn the titles could not be read. And old pew Bibles that had several of the books missing and several troublesome passages simply cut from their pages. (Even several bags of empty toilet paper rolls, each marked with a date and the exact church restroom from which it had come.) These folks are serious about their history. Student workbooks with every blank filled in with ink, broken light fixtures that a junk dealer wouldn't have on his lot, and Sunday school materials whose illustrations pre-dated Ozzie and Harriet were all there. Everything was there! Once a visiting preacher who was "huge of hulk", came to preach a revival, and after the second song when told to be seated, he did and the poor folding chair on the rostrum gave way under him sending him careening into the baptistery. Were there pictures of the event? No, but that poor ol' folding chair was there with all the other sacred junk.

We were later told that Seth and Smitti single-handedly kept an old clapboard meeting house from being torn down for 25 years! Every time the leadership wanted to tear that old heap down to make way for some much needed parking, Seth would rise in a business meeting and filibuster about how precious the heritage of the church was, and how it would be sacrilegious to tear the old shack down. Sacrilegious or not, when the snake and bat count got to epidemic proportions, the city slapped a citation on that place, and unceremoniously brought in a bulldozer and flattened it, with every angelic memory intact. One can only guess where that scrap lumber from that ol' shed got off to in the middle of the night. Never mind that it's latest use had been as a hen house for some stray chickens.

If you doubt that Seth and Smitti were serious about preserving every tangible ounce of anything that had ever been in a church building in that city, it is a well known fact that when they would leave town, the message of their answering machine would say, "Hi, this is Seth. Smitti and I are out of town for a day or two. Rob us if you will, but don't even think about throwing anything from the church away. All clean-up days have hereby been canceled until we get back." The last line didn't always work. Members would live for those times when the Sacredrocks were out of town. Then they would meet at the building en masse, gather up everything that even might need throwing out, and put it all in heavy black trash bags. Then, using an old "seal-a-meal" device they would seal the bags shut, and put them in Barney Newberry's old pick-up, who would then take them 40 miles away to the sanitary landfill of a neighboring town. About sunrise on those joyful mornings the congregation would meet at the Wide Awake Cafe to celebrate their new found space in the buildings and to talk about how Seth and Smitti were going to react when they returned. Seth and Smitti hated those times. Seth said it was enough to make "someone concerned with serious spiritual heritage" curse. But what he hated worse was having to drive 40 miles, and pay $40 to get those black sealed bags back.

When Seth and Smitti moved to their present congregation and presented their "letter", it caused some research to be done. Then, in a clandestine meeting held one night, the church was instructed to "spirit" any worn-out debris, or other trash from the building in the most inconspicuous manner possible and to dispose of it forthwith. Folks, there were women smuggling old hymnals out of there in the stretch panels of maternity wear; Little children forced to hide broken clipboards down the back of their suit coats until they were safely in the car and out of the parking lot; and one brother wound a 50 foot water hose with several holes in it around his upper torso replaced his shirt and started home with it fully concealed. (However...the increased heat caused a garden snake who had taken up residence in the hose, to vacate his housing, which caused the "brother" to suffer a sudden fainting spell and spend three days in the local hospital.)

You may have read various references in Scripture to "not laying up treasures on earth", and even heard sayings like "you can't take it with you"? To this particular brand of "Bottle Baby" whose entire spirituality is wrapped tightly up in "things", not only do they believe every old string bookmark is a treasure, it would seem they think God will allow them to "take it with them". Perhaps they believe God will then turn it all into gold, and pave a street.

9

Eldrod the Elder – Allergic to Sheep

One endearing quality about your average BB is that most of them have no idea that they are, in fact, a "Bottle Baby." So it is with Elrod Eastman and his wife Edora. Elrod was installed as an Elder so many years ago, no one living can truly remember. And truthfully the man is a good man, he's just...well...limited in his perspective of things. Elrod grew up in their little community and he and Edora go all the way back to 2nd grade when she used to throw rocks at poor ol' Elrod on the playground. No one is really sure if it was Edora, or multiplying fractions, that caused Elrod to "give up on book learnin'", but we do occasionally hear him refer to the 5th grade as his "senior year".

When time came to qualify Elrod for the position of local shepherd, there were several hurdles to be overcome. First, while Elrod and Edora had known each other for most of their natural lives, they hadn't always had the smoothest of marriages. More times than anyone wanted to remember Edora had put Elrod's things out on the front porch, and slammed the door hard enough for everyone in six city blocks to hear (luckily they didn't live in the city, but about a mile outside of town, and a quarter mile back off the highway). Anyway, no matter if he was living in the house, or in the barn at the moment, every Sunday the entire family would show up at church. Of course it was pretty obvious to everyone that it was one of "those Sundays", because Elrod would be pulling at his collar, and Edora would be simultaneously blowing the hair out of her eyes, and glaring at the poor man.

Meanwhile all the little Eastman kids would be sitting between them on the pew occasionally rolling their eyes, or looking worried sick. Those children would be Emily, Estelle, Elbert, Elizabeth, Ebeneezer (good biblical name, you know) Eli, and Dude. We all wondered about that little "Dude", strange sort of child. When Dude was in the 3rd grade he was found missing during the dead of night and later reported to have surfaced at the local bar where he "hands down" won the spit'n' and cussin' contest....in every division! But you could really take pride in your Eli. That boy was a natural at science if ever a youngster would be. After he left home and went to the university on a full scholarship in science, he was summarily dismissed for giving the chancellor's wife some "bubble bath" which, when put into warm bath water, would solidify as solid as granite. True it was pretty and blue, and it looked a lot like gelatin, but when that woman poured some in the bath in which she was sitting, it took two jack hammers, and the jaws of life to free her, and the entire ministry department to slap the workers to keep them from folding up laughing on the floor. To be honest it didn't help matters much when they found that the college's "first lady" was going to have a "caboose" permanently dyed periwinkle blue. A color which, I am told, came to evoke spontaneous bursts of laughter from the Chancellor himself.

Then came "poor little Ebeneezer" himself. That poor boy fell out of an ugly tree and hit every limb on the way to the ground. And when he finally got to the ground he landed on his head! Other children wouldn't even attempt to play with the lad. Come to think of it, neither would the family dog "Woofalina" ("Woof", for short). Little Eb used to tell his mama that he wanted to grow up and play second base. However one day as he watched baseball on TV they discovered that he really wanted to *be* second base.

He said it was so that everyone would have to "come by his way to make a score." Today Eb has finally "made it"....well, he works the door at a Las Vegas Nightclub...actually, he's the doorstop. Eb says that it doesn't require much talk, and the pay is real good.

Next is Elizabeth. Phi Beta Kappa at the prestigious Ivy League University. She was voted highest honors in just about every department she attempted in college. Her IQ was documented by several study groups. During her remarks as she received her Ph.D., she told everyone that she was in fact "hatched from a gaggle of rare geese, and raised by Pygmies. And she said she could have never accomplished anything if she hadn't been found by that safari that rescued her. To say that she had severed all ties from the family would be an understatement of rare proportion. No one knows what she has done with all the "annual sweaters" that Edora makes for her each year.

Then you take Elbert. Somebody ought to. Big as the Semi he drives, and twice as noisy. Elbert has the language skills of an arctic seal with a chest cold. Most of his comments are contained in one syllable sounds ...huh..... yah. .. wha?....Donno. And with speech patterns that are low, slow, and with the elasticity of PlayDough, Elbert has made his way in life. Of course when you are 6 foot 5 inches tall and tip the scales at 380 pounds, language just isn't all its piped up to be. Elbert is married to his 4 foot 2 inch wife Ethel, and they have 7 children. Time does not permit me to inventory his family. But Elrod and Edora love everyone of those little "rug rats."

Estelle is the "peach" of her daddy's eye. In reality Elrod loves her, but she's a little "fuzzy" on things, and stays so depressed they often refer to her mental situation as "the pit". Estelle heard, that if you dared, you could make "big bucks" as a "pusher", but try as she might she couldn't find anyone who would let her push their car. The whole thing threw her into a fit , make that a "pit" of depression and she ran off and joined the navy. Her mama is proud to report that her commanding officer said that standing next to those "big guns" when they were being fired, didn't seem to change her powers of concentration at all.

And the first born of the Eastman clan was Emily. Emily was every father's nightmare. Smart, good looking, boy crazy from age 8, cunning, flirtatious, daring....and fast. Early in Emily's life Elrod started seriously reconsidering his decision to quit school in the 5th grade. He needed far more knowledge to just keep up with his daughter who was born at least "two jumps ahead" of ol' dad. I don't know why Elrod's appointment to the leadership should have been questioned by the membership of the church, she had dated most of their sons, and flirted with most of the husbands.

Anyway, you can imagine the sort of questions that came up when Elrod's name was put before the congregation. The final assessment was that although he and Edora hadn't always gotten along, they had "stuck it out".

And even though his kids were "wild as March hares" he did do his best to have them "in submission", although there was doubt that a legion of angels could have handled a couple of them.

The terminology that was most often used was "he's a good man". That is church code for "not one of us has the guts to tell him he can't serve".

Elrod had recently retired from his powerful post at the feed lot where he commanded a team of 12 "lot sweeps", yes that is exactly what you think it means. Anyway, his new found freedom boded very well at home for a couple of weeks, until it dawned on Elrod that he no longer had anyone to "boss". He certainly wasn't going to "boss" Edora, she would surely put a knot on his head and send him to the barn. His kids weren't exactly going to "line up for inspection" when he spoke. So Elrod figured out that since he was an Elder he could "boss" the local preacher. And "boss" him he did. It is indeed a difficult undertaking to try to "boss" someone who is doing a job that one has not a clue about, but Elrod tried anyway. Back when he was working at the feedlot Elrod had to "balance the books" (that meant count the cows and see if the number was the same on the tally sheet) so now he decided that the church budget would be his personal project. Every meeting was filled with questions about the budget, and foreboding projections of "hard times" ahead.

His favorite money saying was "you know, when it's gone, it's gone", and everyone would nod in amazement. Somewhere, someone had led Elrod to believe that God had taken Chapter 11, and was now living in public housing on food stamps. It always puzzled Elrod as to what happened to those "cattle on a thousand hills", he would remark from time to time, "now that must have been some really hard times!"

Elrod probably reached the zenith of his shepherding career when the congregation was contemplating buying new pew cushions for the sanctuary.

The old ones were run down and the wrong color, and the new carpet would really look better with new ones that matched. Elrod was, as usual, more concerned with the financial side of things. After several weeks of debates on the pew cushions, Elrod suddenly blurted out a non-financial statement that has mesmerized those who were in attendance ever since. He said "You know what wears them cushions out, don't you?" Well, every eye looked his way, every ear perked up to hear, and all talking on lesser things stopped.

Elrod was at his finest moment. He proceeded. "I'll tell you what wears them things out....its them old women passin' gas through 'em". Well, birds stopped singing, and water ran up hill for a while there, as everyone took in the genius of that statement. Someone must have had a look on their face that asked the silent question "Why?", because Elrod went on. "You know what those pads are made of don't ya? Urine-thane! That's why that gas reacts with it and makes them go flat!" At that point the meeting pretty much broke up. Elrod sauntered out the door, while the rest of the men present lay on the floor laughing so hard they could not breathe. If Edora had been there she would have "Took him up side the head" with her purse and muttered those familiar words, "Oh Elll-rod!"

A man in that position in the church is required by scripture to be a "people-person", that is a shepherd of the sheep. Elrod was a little shy in that department. He did pretty good among the "ram lambs", that would be the men of the congregation, but when he was confronted by Mary Beth Honnibunch or any of the other ladies, he turned to a quivering mass of Jello in their very midst. The Ladies (Ewe lambs) knew that if they wanted to do any serious bickering or complaining Elrod was their man. He would stand there and listen to a mad woman for hours even if she was trying to convince him that the Red Sea was held back by special effects and props. Elrod just didn't know what to do, and Edora certainly hadn't given him much room for assertiveness at home.

As Elrod got older, all of these misgivings and lack of credentials began to cause him great concern. Edora needed for him to be an Elder so she could maintain her clout in the feminine pecking order, but every time someone mentioned his children he found it hard to raise his eyes from the ground.

So he did the only thing he could do: he became bitter. His remarks to members were short and sharp. And nothing that ever happened at church was "right" or "good enough", until it had been proven so, and then Elrod would suddenly decide it was all "his idea". Actually, we all knew that it wasn't, it had "Edora" stamped all over it.

A few months ago ol' Elrod died in his sleep. At the funeral were all of his seven kids and his 26 grandchildren. (four apiece except for Emily) On the day of his passing Edora had called the local monument works and ordered a beautiful headstone and had it engraved "Rest in peace". About noon she discovered that two weeks before ol' Elrod had taken their entire savings and put down on a new lawn tractor which he hid out in the shed, and which was now being used to cut the lawn so the house would look nice for the funeral.

The lady of the Eastman house hit the ceiling! She called that monument works and demanded that the inscription be changed. (to what, I don't know.) However, she was told that once it was engraved she was the owner of the monument. So the "Rest In Peace" would have to stay. Eldora asked if something could be added, and she was told that certainly it could, she said in a voice that wasn't as controlled as she would have liked, "put...until we meet again."" Elrod, ill equipped for the job of shepherd, is laying under six feet of Oklahoma dirt, and it's quite possibly the first really calm rest he's had in years.

10

Sharon the Shower Lady

In the course of every year, of every church you have ever heard of, there are certain events such as weddings, births, divorces, and an occasional death that call for a "shower" of some description. And that is when a mysterious phenomenon takes place: Sharon Giftbox and her husband George suddenly announce that such a "shower" has been planned and "you are all invited".

Actually George could be eliminated from this whole activity except that Sharon always wears her best dress with the straight skirt and she can't unload the Studebaker without George. So at most of these events, George sets up the tables, puts on the tablecloths, sets out the glassware, puts out the silverware, the punchbowl, and the nut tray, and then, realizing he is the only male on the premises, he retires behind a stack of folding tables to sit in a straight chair and talk to himself until the shower is over.

Sharon Giftbox is a master at figuring out "just the right" theme and place for each shower, sometimes before she has even met the honoree. And of course, after all these events she is the hands down queen of what is "precious" and "cute". And let it be known she can make a circle of chairs anywhere. If you put this woman in a rat maze and turned out the light, when the lights came on, she would have a circle of chairs. That is, of course, because "square is tacky", and anything else just "looks funny". Sharon's real talents come out when she is making – more like "concocting" – , the punch for each of these celebrations. Ginger Ale, pineapple juice, white grape juice, crushed pineapple, and 7-up and a little food color, and Voila! ol' Sharon can make any kind of punch she thinks you ought to have.

There was that dreadful day when a newcomer to the congregation, Gale Gatelowe, decided that she would put on a shower herself for the next appropriate occasion and "take a little stress" off of Sis. Sharon. This unfortunate happening is why, to this day, Gale is known as "little miss stick her nose in it" to many of the women in the church. To be sure Sharon and all her buddies were present at Gale's shower. They all walked in wearing their dark business suits with pearls, sat at attention never peering to either right or left, talking to no one and never a smile or smallest chuckle ever crossed their lips. The effect was something like trying to build a signal fire under a blanket full of snow. As Sharon and her lieutenants rose to leave each of them was heard to make at least one remark about Gale's event: "That punch didn't have enough taste to it", "Weren't those cookies a little underdone?" "Where did they get those decorations? Out of someone's basement?" And on it went until each one of them had demeaned Gale's attempt. "Demeaned" is a good word for it, for when they are mad those are de-meanest bunch of women that ever sat a pew. Little did they know, that Gale had been forewarned about "Sharon's legions", and she had played some really bad games at first, and those soda cookies were indeed terrible. However, the plan worked, for as soon as Sharon and the others left, the real party got under way. The "good stuff" that had been hiding in the store room under Saran-wrap came out, and everyone had a wonderful time. However, to complete the ruse, every time they saw Sharon during the next month, they would just purse their lips and shake their heads and walk on by her. Sharon thought her legions were growing. So far, in the past ten years, that whole charade has been repeated for Sharon's benefit at least 15 times.

No one down at the church will soon forget the time that Sharon planned that grand baby shower for the Drumroll baby. Well, the little boy was suppose to be due in about three weeks, but Mother Nature decided to get the little guy to earth about three days before the scheduled shower. Well, Sharon hadn't seen the little tike – they named him Sylvester, but I think they are going to call him "Sticks" – anyway she had thought up all the "cutest" games, and even broke out some "darling" songs, and went "all the way" and got some party favors that would be "fun" to take home afterward. Interestingly enough, most of the planned activities necessitated showing pictures of little "Sticks Drumroll" to make the games work. The problem arose when his mother , Ruth Drumroll, came in to the applause of the large gathering of ladies and whipped the blanket back so everyone could get their first look at little "Sticks". It was enough to make everyone stop in mid- "oooh", and choke so the "Ahh" sounded more like "Iyaya". That was the ugliest baby every seen on planet earth. I don't mean that the poor child just had the usual marks of birthing, I mean that child looked like the doctor delivered him with a pair of track shoes. First, he had red hair...well, actually orange hair was more like it, and it was arranged by mother nature so that he could be the stand-in for the troll dolls they were giving away at Whataburger. It was later reported that at his birth three people ran out of the room, one to laugh out loud, one who was mad at his mother, and one to call Ripley's Believe it or Not.

You can imagine the kink that threw in Sharon's plan. She had a game where there were several baby pictures, and all the women were supposed to "defer" to the new mother by picking the picture of "Sticks". That turned out to be pretty difficult to pull off since a ground mole would have picked the snapshot of a hedgehog pup over "lil Sticks". And when they got to the place where Sharon was supposed to put "Sticks" picture on some frozen dessert bars, she just couldn't bear to kill everyone's appetite, so she left the pictures off. To say that things got a "little tense" would be a "oh-not-true" statement.

One at a time the ladies quietly disappeared out the most convenient exit. Which left Sharon, Ruth Drumroll, Little Sticks, and George. Remember George? He was sitting over behind that stack of tables half asleep, and when the crowd sort of thinned to the consistency of wax paper, Sharon suddenly woke him up and ordered him to "come look at this precious baby". George took one look and fainted dead away right then and there. It was a disaster!

The only redeeming part of this disaster was that the mother got to take the entire double sheet cake home and eat it herself. From that day forward Sharon never gave another shower without requiring a picture of any baby that was going to be brought to the event, and she preferred pictures from more than one angle.

You have to give credit. Sharon and George have at their house a large steamer trunk with all sorts of gifts in it suitable for showers. Most of that stuff Sharon has gotten from showers she attended before she ascended the throne as the Shower lady. She has not, to date, ever given a gift at a shower to the mother that gave her that gift, but the anticipation of that time grows with each passing year. And here's hoping that Sharon realizes at last that the "shower" is for the other person, and not a competitive sport.

11

Bubba the Board Member

Theodore "Bubba" Letitslide was actually elected to the board of First Church above the concerns and objections of the Good Lord and of his wife, Lotty. First of all, Lotty said that Bubba just didn't have time to be on the church board and spend even a little time with their kids: Les, Lucrita, Lolita, Lenard, and Proba Lee. (That's right, they named that kid Proba Lee Letitslide) However, when Bubba's name came up for consideration, he literally jumped at the chance. In retrospect, some of the members are just sure that he was pushed.

Lotty Letitslide is the sort of woman that runs her family, her home, and most of North America with a firm hand, and an iron will. That's is probably why Bubba found that sitting on the church board gave him a handy venue for expressing his pent-up opinions on several subjects near to his heart.

Bubba did have some problems "getting the hang of it" at first. When the local football team was about to play for the state championship, Bubba opened that week's board meeting with a prayer that included a line about God causing their opponent's team to be struck with nausea and diarrhea. Folks, Bubba can't even pronounce "diarrhea." After the stares from that comment had finally faded away, and the heads had stopped shaking, Bubba opened the meeting with an item that wasn't on the agenda for the meeting. He rose to his feet and said "What are we going to do about the toilet paper problem?" Well, in all honesty, no one else knew there was a "toilet paper problem" so the chair person of the evening asked Bubba what exactly that might be. Bubba said, with great conviction and intonation, "Splinters!" The entire board immediately voted to ask the custodian to upgrade the bathroom paper at the first convenient moment.

While Bubba delighted, and almost swooned, to see his name on the documents that emitted from the board from time to time, he never could completely perceive that his was a stewardship role and not one of command. That perception caused quite a problem since Bubba couldn't grasp most of the questions that came before the board. So, Bubba would sit in silence and try to decide who would vote for what, so that he could always get in on the winning side. In the process of practicing that little technique he learned to say certain "religious sounding things", like asking "does this have a scriptural implication?" or perhaps interjecting into the conversation that "there are far reaching implications to this matter that might need further scrutiny." He was being honest. Any implication that was more than 24 hours, or 3 feet, in the future was "far reaching" from Bubba's perspective. Bubba even found that there were certain things that the board was called on to decide that were so explosive in nature (his mother-in-law and his wife didn't agree) that he would mumble quickly under his breath "I-refrain-from-votin'". No one could understand him completely, so they would skip him and take the rest of the vote.

Bubba's lack of understanding also caused the board to hold meetings in such a tone and vocabulary that most Philadelphia lawyers could not understand. The obvious idea was "what Bubba doesn't know, he can't vote on".

One of the board's many duties that caught Bubba totally off guard was the dismissing and calling of clergy. Bubba Letitslide found himself in the position of casting the final and deciding vote to dismiss their pastor, and his head swelled with pride to know that it was he who would deliver the history making vote. That night he went home feeling ten feet tall and bullet proof, until he got home and found that the news of his vote had gotten there first. Then Bubba found out that he had just fired the first and only pastor that his wife and all his kids had liked since they moved their letter to First Church.

After one of the most brutal family meetings and impromptu devotionals in history, Bubba found himself drawn between his family who was about to write him out of the will, and trying to change the mind of the board when it was he who had delivered that fateful vote. To say that Bubba was "between a rock and a hard place" is to understate the situation completely. Lotty was about to move his clothes to the garage permanently, along with an old mattress for him to sleep on, and the board was ready to cut him off at the proxy until Bubba got what possibly may be the most inspired idea of his life. He sat in the next board meeting and told the board that he had "received a directive", direct from God, in the form of a vision, and he had heard "a voice" so he "just must" change his vote. Now, how could that board argue with such high and heavenly reasoning? And wouldn't any church person worth their own pew do the same if they had received such a revelation? So the board changed their vote, the pastor stayed, Bubba moved back into the house, and the board started having "executive meetings" at some undisclosed location at times when Bubba couldn't possibly be present. The Pastor had even thanked Bubba profusely, and assured him that he must be a righteous person to have heard such voice from God. Actually, most of the congregation was pretty sure it was that plate of Burritos, and the popcicle that he had eaten before going to bed the night before.

Things only got more exciting during the month that Bubba became acting "chair" of the board. That was when Bubba showed up at a meeting wearing a T-shirt emblazoned with the words "The Board – rocks!" obviously Bubba was diving deep into the shallow end of his mind. And it was during his tenure as "chair" that the "crying baby problem" was addressed, as was the "strong perfume problem", not to mention "going overtime in worship problem." Bubba would just "inspire" such discussions on these matters that some of the meetings lasted into the wee hours of the morning. Actually Bubba couldn't have cared less. His kids were no longer babies, his wife never did wear strong perfume, and Bubba slept through the service, so he considered it "more rest on the Lord's Day". His fellow board members did not hold such lackadaisical opinions on these subjects. Especially Clem Combs whose wife, Clementine, bought her perfume wholesale from a chemical company along with her industrial strength hairspray. And to top it all off Clementine had produced for Clem (far into his middle age years) an offspring, just about every year, so that "baby" business really hit close to home.

It is reported that the board actually gave Bubba the responsibility of taking care of the flower boxes along the front of First Church. They assured Bubba that he didn't need a vote, nor a meeting for that matter, just "do whatever you think is appropriate." Well, how fortunate for all concerned that Bubba and Lotty were leaving on vacation the very next morning. The Letitslides were going to take a car tour across the Southern United States. Somewhere along the way Bubba discovered this very hardy variety of ivy that seemed to thrive everywhere it was planted. Its rich green, not to mention huge leaves were luxuriant everywhere they looked. Well, you guessed it, Bubba seeded those flower boxes with Kudzu Vine. It was the first time that anyone at First Church or in the community as a whole had ever seen Kudzu, but not for long. Before the spring had ended that vine had totally covered the front of First church, run along the ground to a near by junk yard, completely encasing the wrecked cars there, and taken over two oak trees over forty feet in height.

The town council was called to "see who the numbskull was who had introduced such a noxious vine in to their community". Well, every breathing person on that board knew...it was Bubba. After having this "slight miscalculation" called to his attention, Bubba then started "thinkin'", that is, he did nothing , just thought about what he might do. By the time the Kudzu reached the courthouse lawn, the whole town planned this "torchlight parade" right to Bubba's house. There they found Bubba on the front porch wearing a navy blue T-Shirt emblazoned with the words "Procrastinate – -Now !" Every man, woman and child in that assembly turned around and went home. Bubba was summarily relieved of his duties on the board, and Lotty is still shaking her head and clucking her tongue at the man to this very day.

12

Fred the Pharisee – Keeper of Fringe and Phylacteries

Fred Fontaine and his wife Fredonia, or "Shorty" as she was known, came to the local church having been raised in one of those congregations where "everything is suspicious, and we aren't sure about anybody". Over the years Shorty had made a career out of correcting Fred's every move and grooming him to be one of the "chief" men in the congregation. Shorty had even written away for a ten lesson Bible course from a school down in Texas, complete with two full length video tapes so that Fred could be thoroughly educated to assume the position of teacher in the local church. Those video tapes never did do Fred much good. At first they did not own a VCR , and when they did finally purchase one, "Shorty" never could get the thing to play. Just as well, for when Fred would go to the church building to watch his tapes, he would get into arguments with the TV screen that were so loud the secretary finally asked him to only come to the building at night "When no one is here to hear you." However, Fred persevered...and it's a good thing because "Shorty" would quiz him at breakfast every morning about what he had learned. She'd say "Fred tell me what you know about the role of women in the church in Bible times." And Fred would answer, "they were told to sit there and keep their mouths shut! And if they wanted to know anything ask their husbands." "Shorty" would then roll up a newspaper and slap Fred across the side of his head, reminding him that she was the exception to that rule and he best not forget it.

"Sister Fontaine", as she was called by those who were scared more of her than a rattlesnake, was the proudest woman on planet earth the day her husband was made one of the leaders of the congregation. Not that she had any fantasies about ol' Fred actually being qualified nor ready, she just saw this as her opportunity to "get a few things straightened out" that were bothering her.

Fred had faithfully watched and taken notes on those two video tapes, so he could stand in a Bible class and at least discuss the books of Song of Solomon and Jude. The language of Song of Solomon caused him to blush, so he never really got around to teaching that class. But he was a whiz on Jude.

After it became obvious that the whole church knew he wasn't literate, much less versed on anything else, Fred started suggesting that "after all his many years of teaching (that would be four) he felt that he should take himself out of the teaching rotation and let some of the younger men take over". Well, that was a surprise throughout the universe. Seriously, God was surprised since the Bible said that the man should be the teacher, and Fred's name wasn't mentioned anywhere as the exception, and the congregation was surprised since they thought they would never be delivered from Fred's classes.

One thing that Fred was adamant about was being against anything "new".

The first time it was suggested that perhaps the scholarship was better in one of the newer translations of the Bible, Fred was the first to stand and say "As long as I'm a leader in this church, we'll stay with the "St. James version! Around here we don't need any of that Reversed Vision!" The simplicity of that remark sort of stands by itself. Then Fred had pronouncements on about everything that came along, including the songs that the church would sing. When new music was suggested, Fred would stand and solemnly say "The songs in the song book were good enough for the Apostle Paul and my dear mother, and they are good enough for me!" That may have been true, because there IS some evidence that Paul stuttered, we all knew that his dear mother was tone deaf, and Fred couldn't carry the bucket a tune went in. Finally, over the objections of Fred and Shorty, who mounted a mighty female tirade against it all, the congregation bought new song books, and one of those projection devises that projected the words to the song on the front wall of the building. Fred, it would seem, was about to have a "rigor". Fred would smile from ear to ear anytime the new machinery didn't work. He was quick to point out that there were "700 songs in those new books, and we don't sing but 50 of 'em". (Of course they had only had the books for two weeks)

Fred totally forgot to mention the fact, that not only could he not sing, he didn't sing...he just chose to not open his mouth. That gave him ample time to be looking around during the song service for other things that needed attention. Those "other things" often turned out to be the children of young couples who "just need to learn how to discipline them and keep them quiet in God's house". Or it might have been some other brother or sister who was nodding off just a bit. Fred would say "It is a disgrace the way they sleep in service! If they want to sleep let them stay home!" All of that sounded pretty good until the sermon started and Fred would prop up a song book in his lap and lean at just the right angle to make one think he was reading the Bible, and then take "just a short nap". This brought on a situation the congregation will never forget. One Sunday, little six year old Orson Fishbeck was sitting directly behind Bro. Fred. Well, Fred had just gotten "really comfortable" when Orson leaned over to asked his dad how long it would be until "that man tells us to stand and sing". Only just as Orson got to the words "Stand and sing" his sister poked him with a ball point pen. Orson really came out with those three words "Stand and Sing!" which woke Fred up, and upon hearing those words did, in fact, stand and sing. Well, it fairly ruined the sermon, Shorty was just mortified, and ol' Fred had to retire his "No sleeping in church" sermon forever.

Because Fred was of the Pharisee persuasion, neither the big major events at church, nor the clearest of bible teachings, bothered him much. He was the tightest of the tightwad benevolence people, actually getting to the point of being able to cower the poor and homeless into giving him money. He was highly suspicious of fellowship meals because he said it resembled "entertainment" to him. Of course he went. Fred loved all the good cooking, and beside it was Shorty's only opportunity to show off her "killer baked beans". Only baked beans in history that were so thick and gooey that the mayor asked her for her recipe so they could pave a street with them. Shorty would not miss an opportunity to make those beans, so Fred got to go to the fellowships.

Actually Fred was pretty "suspicious" of anything that looked like "entertainment". He fought having a youth minister for years on the basis of "we aren't paying someone to just entertain our kids!" Pretty tall talk for a man with only one son. And "lil' Fonzy" had left home several years ago vowing to never return.

Puppet ministries, youth camps, Vacation Bible Schools that served Kool-aid, pizza parties, and over night lock-ins were all looked down on by Fred and Shorty as just pure "entertainment". Like so many other things they opposed, neither Fred nor Shorty had ever been to any of the above mentioned functions, and surely would never volunteer to do so.

Fred had, however, gone bowling once. Therefore "bowling is just good wholesome entertainment".

Of course Fred also looked down on all those Bible conferences, and evangelism workshops too. He said they were just "church political conventions, and every time someone sneezes there the whole church catches cold." Actually, that wasn't his real motive. Fred knew that if he attended he might see what was happening elsewhere in "Christendom" and be embarrassed at what he was doing. AND, he was afraid that some of that added education would surely mess up his set of opinions and outlooks on the scripture. Fred would read the reports of such meetings and shake his head while muttering in a reverent tone, "The mind is a terrible thing...". One summer Fred even undertook to make a list of all the "suspect" preachers and teachers in his brotherhood. Then he decided that he would include all the "suspect" institutions of higher learning. Well, it finally came down to the point that just about anyone who knew more than Song of Solomon and Jude were "suspect" in Fred's mind. Actually Fred did find a couple of people he felt were possibly "sound", but in reality he was even a little unsure about them.

After taking himself out of the teaching rotation, since everyone had already heard his two lessons on "the Song" and Jude, Fred had to find something else to occupy his time. So he decided on a couple of things. First, he would be the monitor of "church conduct during worship", and second, he would be the authority on the "wise use of God's money". This "conduct during worship" thing was really going to cut into his Sunday morning naps, but Fred thought that this was significant. Since the Bible has very little to say about "slouching in worship" or "laughing in worship", or "telling funny stories in sermons" Fred was sure to have little if any opposition when he positioned his opinions as scriptural fact. "I just believe that all the illustrations in sermons should come from the Bible and leave all those outside things alone" he would intone to anyone who was dull enough to listen. Finally one day someone pointed out that the parables were just "everyday illustrations" that Jesus used, and some of them were even funny to that audience. Did that make a difference? Nooooo! You see, one of the main tenants of the Pharisaical mind is to "fill in the blanks" on anything God hasn't specifically said. Well, that left ol' Fred with a variable smorgasbord of topics on which to pronounce judgment. And if Fred wasn't quick enough to pick up on some area that needed correction, Shorty was. She was the real force behind Fred's quest on these matters. You see Fredonia "Shorty" Fontaine, in the deep reaches of her beehive hairdo, really believed that she was actually a man, and therefore destined to be a leader in the local church. Problem was she couldn't pass the physical. So Shorty just mentally grabbed ol' Fred by the ears, and much like one would use a bull horn in a mob, pronounced her opinions through him. One daring young preacher actually made mention of the fact that this was exactly the practice that the Apostle Paul condemned in the Book of First Corinthians. Well, when he said Paul was preaching against "loud mouthed, self-willed ol' women" he probably went a little far. To say the least, he didn't stay long at the church. Shorty took it personally and went into a major "huff".

There was only one eventuality that brought dread to the heart of every member of that congregation, and that is when Shorty wouldn't have Fred anymore to use as her surrogate in the leadership. After all Shorty was 22 years Fred's junior. So most could see a woman in the future who had swayed the church repeatedly through her husband, who now was alone and bitter, and basically unheeded. A frightful specter to say the least. Something like pulling a 220 volt cord loose from inside the wall and turning on the breaker with it attached to nothing. What ever got in her way was likely to be severely burned.

Several of the ladies of the church had tried to "quite" Shorty down. They softly suggested that maybe she should concentrate on some of the good things happening in the church, and leave the controversial things alone. One even suggested that Shorty might start each day with saying something good about one of the members, writing a positive note to a member, and calling a member to inquire about how they were doing. Shorty heard the organization of this "three-pronged approach," she just didn't "get" all the details. So each morning she would get up and say to Fred "You ain't much, but at least you are better than.....(whoever the victim of the day was)!" Then she would sit down and write a note telling some woman how "if it were her, she would slap her teen age daughter silly, the next time she wore that skirt to church..." And finally she would call up some other woman and tell her she had better "get started trying to get her husband to church before he went straight to hell!" This tactic traumatized the church, but it sure made Shorty feel better.

Some said she probably would have just divorced ol' Fred, but he was her mouthpiece in the men's meetings, and besides she had been pretty stout on her stand about divorce.

One of the tell-tale signs about the Phariseeism that ran rampant in Fred and Shorty's house was that it was obvious to everyone that the rules from the Bible, nor the rules of common decency did not apply to them. They could say whatever they wanted to, to whoever they wanted to, and never even expect anyone to react. Sometimes they could just lie, in a holy sort of way of course. And Fred became quite adept at taking bits and pieces of scripture and using them to sound holy as he lambasted someone else's opinion. It was interesting that after Fred had used some of that "paper-mache' scripture" he could never again change his position on that subject, no matter how much scripture in context he might be shown. In case you don't know what "paper-mache' Scripture is" it is scraps of Bible that have no connection to each other, held together with the glue of pure hudspa.

That is why Fred never tried to enter the arena of Biblical study. He stayed mostly in the realm of "judgmental matters" and of course financial matters.

As "God's right hand man" he felt fully qualified to decide how "God's money was going to be spent". And besides, accounting for the money took up so much time that he would never have to worry about such mundane things as the spiritual well-being of the other members, or the spiritual future of the congregation. "Just keep the church out of the red" was his battle cry. Fred was so sure that he would be allowed to take the church treasury and the books with him that he arranged to have pockets put in his burial suit. (Shorty bought him a new suit for when the occasion would arise, because she didn't want to mess up her million dollar garage sale by burying one of his good suits) And Fred also to had a trailer hitch put on the hearse so they could bury him with the things that were truly significant to him in life. Fred used to say, with great magnificence and aplomb, "one day I'll see you all at judgment!" Personally, I think that is debatable, but if we do see him you will be able to recognize him. Fred will be the one with the eyes wide as saucers, and that surprised look on his face. He will be arguing with God to let him sit in one of the "big chairs at the front so things will be done right", while Shorty is there at his side whining and murmuring about "how in the world some of these people even got here in the first place!" And then all will see the fruition of an old saying....what goes around will come around.

13

Darrell The Deacon

It was thirteen years ago when the leaders of the local congregation came to Darrell Drumroll and asked him to serve as a deacon in the congregation. After checking with his wife Demitria (nicknamed "Dimmy") Darrell decided to "give it a whirl". Also suddenly being cast into the limelight as part of the deacon's family were all the Drumroll kids: Three boys, Dennis, Dwane, and Buck, and two girls, Dominex and Star. All of the Drumroll siblings were remarkable for their age, well, all but little Buck. "Lit'l Buck", as he was known, was the reason most preacher's kids get talked about: they hang out with deacon's kids like Lit'l Buck. If ever soap got thrown in the fountain in front of First Church, or if a stink bomb was ever set off in the basement, or if someone wrote naughty words on the rock fence in front of Mary Beth Hunnibunch's house, there was not a question asked, they just went and got Lit'l Buck. Darrell always reacted the same, he'd start every sentence with "Boy!"

Such as,"Boy! I swear I don't know what we are gonna do with you! I guess I'm just gonna have to keep whippin' you until I beat you death and then let the Lord handle you!" Meanwhile Demitria would stand by quietly saying

"Now Darrell, Now Darrell.." Lit'l Buck knew that this was all just part of the "show" put on for the benefit of the brethren, because the unspoken rule was always "Buck didn't do it! I don't know who did, but it wasn't Buck!"

However, you did have to give Darrell credit for having a lot of "get up and go" when it came to his duties as a deacon. Darrell was first assigned to the task of taking care of the physical property of the church. After Demitria explained "that does not mean hugging all the ladies", Darrell went after the job, in earnest. When the parking lot needed repairing, Darrell "jumped right on it", hiring the highest paid, and least experienced contractor that he could possibly find. And while that parking lot looked wonderful, the church took up extra love offerings for a month to pay for the thing. Then someone mentioned that the drapes in the back of the pulpit were looking rather shabby. Ordinarily some of the ladies of the church, or Mary Beth Hunnibunch and her band of henchwomen, would have taken care of such things, but Darrell simply beat them to it. Darrell thought that he would add a little personality to the place by having those drapes made from that "gold sparkly material", so the church found themselves with Gold Lame' drapes, which Darrell immediately saw would never match the tired and worn old carpet, so he had that changed to a brilliant royal purple. And since the brown pew cushions just wouldn't do, he had them done in snow white. Now dear reader, feature what we have here, as the members file in for Sunday worship at First Church : we have purple carpet, with white seat cushions, and Gold "sparkly" drapes. Some suspected Darrell got his inspiration from the Circus, while others were highly suspicious that Darrell had seen the inside of some of the houses in the red light district.

Well, as you might imagine the leadership called Darrell in and chastised him severely for all this, to which Darrell replied, "Look you gave me this job, and you told me to take care of it myself, and now I have done the best I can, and all I get from you is grief!" That argument is pretty hard to refute when you think about it, so everyone agreed to allow Darrell to keep his assignment.

Darrell was just a "hair" gun-shy now, so he took far too much time in making decisions, and had to be prodded to do the simplest things around the building.

So the tile in the ladies bathroom went a year before being fixed, the sign out front like to have "never" gotten painted. And, generally, Darrell was "snake bit", and had fallen into the rut of those who had gone before him of doing nothing until he was told at least ten times. That is, until the church mini van needed painting. The little vehicle had barely five-hundred-thousand-miles on it when it was decided that since junk dealers kept bothering the church secretary with offers to "haul it off", it needed a coat of paint. Darrell, now far too obsessed with "how much things cost", decided to take it to the local Vocational School and enlist the help of their auto-body class for the project.

In that class were juvenile delinquents from three different decades, and some who had already enjoyed the hospitality of the state police on a number of occasions. As they talked to Darrell they all came to understand that he was indeed "Cool", and a someone they liked. And Darrell was also someone they could talk into a-n-y-thing. So, you can imagine the delight of the youth group, and the nausea of the older members, when Darrell drove into the parking lot with a 72 minivan painted Pepto-Bismol Pink with white "lightening stripes" down each side. The bumpers and all the insignias on the vehicle were painted metallic purple (a little darker than the carpet in the building) and the interior had been done in rolls-and-pleats of royal purple and white. To sort of finish off this "masterpiece" the van now sported tires wide enough to fill an entire traffic lane by themselves, and hub caps of baked on Gold enamel.

Oh yes, and to make the little van more "hip", Darrell had added a white "spoiler" to the top rear of it all. To say the least, the reception to this new paint job was "mixed". Some said that Darrell had really added some "joy" to the JOY BUS. Others said it looked like the driver needed a white suit with a huge white Panama hat. In hushed tones, always with a snicker, the kids referred to it as the "pimp-mobile". And everyone wondered how long it would last after Darrell, took the ladies of the bible class on an outing to a nearby mall, and had five different people came up to the van and asked if he was selling "watches", and if not, did he have any drugs they could buy. Probably asking Mary Beth Hunnibunch "how's tricks" didn't speak highly of the reaction the van was drawing. Darrell defended all of these things, and his paint job too, by mentioning that "we sure didn't have any trouble finding our bus in a parking lot at youth rallies". And the leadership had to agree that they were having an unusual influx of younger people at church all of a sudden.

I guess the end of Darrell's term as deacon came when he was asked to place a new sign on a large open area of the building, so people coming down the main street could plainly see where First Church was located. Darrell went into a major "be sure about everything, nit-picking, frenzy" over the whole project, he called in designers, contacted paint manufacturers about how long their paint would last, and actually drove to several wood mills to see about different building materials and how long they would endure in that climate.

You can only imagine the look in Darrell's eyes, when one Sunday morning he drove up to the building and found that someone had already painted a sign right on the side of that building without even asking him. It seems one of the leader's cousin-in-laws had gone into the sign business and had been told to "just go ahead". Darrell was furious! He walked into a meeting of the leadership, catching them in the middle of an intense discussion over the cost of different grades of toilet paper, and threw his keys on the desk. He told them in a voice that was loud and agitated, "If you are going to give me a job to do, then let me do it! And you don't seem to think much of my skill so I quit.!" There was a moment of stunned silence, after which someone said "OK", and they went back to the "toilet paper matter".

The entire ugly matter scarred Darrell and Demitria up something terrible. For days Demitria moped around the house and periodically cried and whimpered about how Darrell had been "done wrong". But it was "Lit'l Buck" that took it hardest. Buck was now 13 and everyone said he was on his way to greatness as a plate maker at the local prison. No one knows for sure how it happened, but some how, that sign that read "First Church Sanctuary" suddenly came to read "First Circus of Sanctimony" and there on the lower right hand corner was the name of the cousin-in-law for all the world to see. And Darrell, well, Darrell is still faithful in his attendance at First Church, and is the best teacher of, and foremost authority on, the book of First Opinions.

14

Alfred Altizer, the All American Christian

It seems that no matter when you walk in the building of First Church you will find Alfred Altizer or his wife Trish. You see for the past 15 years every time someone has deserted the educational program, either Alfred or Trish has quickly stepped in to take up the slack. Trish has often been heard to say "I know teaching four classes every Sunday is hard, but somebody has got to see that the material is covered."

It would be seemingly impossible for two people to do all the things that the Altizers do from week to week. There are those four classes that Alfred keeps running. Trish is the "teacher of record" on all the classes from Kindergarten through 5th grade. Then Alfred steps into the parking lot in time to drive the bus to pick up folks down at Specimen Bottle Manor, the local nursing facility. All of that has to be done so that Alfred can get those folks back to the building, park the bus, and slip into "his pew" just as the first hymn is about to be sung. "Ms. Trish", as the kids call her, is meanwhile doing her own "thing" keeping her own three children Al, Allyson, and Allissa all under control along with 14 bus children who were brought in before class started that morning. Of course, it is somewhat helpful that Ms. Trish possesses a talent of "pinching the soft underside of the arm (you know the part that hangs down on old folks) with such "pressure per square inch" that truck drivers have been known to have their eyes fairly bulge from the pain. And Alfred has an "ear thump" that will leave your head ringing internally for hours.

Once Alfred corrected one of the bus kids, one LaShawn Jones, with just such a "ear thump". Turned out that LaShawn had ears built like the mudflaps on an eighteen wheeler and when that ear got to moving at such a rate two of the older ladies sitting to his right almost froze to death because of the wind it stirred up.

None of this highly choreographed dedication could have taken place if Alfred wasn't a master in talking folks who wanted to quit into "being his assistant teacher". Somewhere there really should be a plaque for Alfred as one of the world's greatest motivators of weak Sunday School teachers.

Add to all this confusion of intense dedication, the fact that it was Trish's job to fix the communion service each Sunday, and Alfred to "take the Official Count" of how many folks were in church. All of these duties and chores often made the Altizers look a lot like that little squirrel that pops up and down at the arcade while you try to hit it with a big hammer. When He's up, she's down, and visa-versa. One Sunday the preacher was going to quiz them at the door about his own sermon, but when he saw the heavy-breathing and perspiration pouring off of them like sweat, he simply didn't have the heart. Besides, for that quiz of his to have been very long he would have had to run along side the church's minivan as it moved out of the church parking lot.

Well, we all knew that one day it would happen, we feared it, we dreaded it, and it was just something you didn't talk about without causing serious doubts. However, one Sunday, Alfred and Trish "just weren't quite on their game". I mean they were "out of sinc" just a tad. Alfred was starting a class on Samson and all that business with the jaw bone of an ass, and then he would "turn it over" to his assistant teacher and go to the next class where they were studying Noah and the Ark. Well, that particular morning, neither of the assistant teachers showed up. And after passing between those two classes about six or eight times, you would not believe how "fouled up" those Bible stories got. It seems that Alfred had Samson with two jaw bones, loading animals two-by-two onto a speedboat, while Noah got angry with "Ham Shem, and Japhath and paddled their ....well, you know.

Things weren't going any better with Trish. She had gotten to church late, meaning, that the three classes of pre-schoolers she was watching and teaching were enjoying a hearty breakfast of white paste and crayolas by the time she arrived. (Their parents "couldn't stay, you understand" because keeping those little classes was "somebody else's job"). Anyway, all of that cut into her time in preparing the communion trays for that morning. Trish was so rushed that she inadvertently reached for the "Welch's best purple grape juice (on sale at the local IGA for forty cents off) and instead got hold of the bottle of persimmon wine that Herb Newton, the church janitor, had stashed in the back of the fridge. She quickly filled the trays without really looking at what she was doing, then she blew the crumbs from the unleavened bread left in the trays from the Sunday before, and "she was ready". But I am fairly certain that the church wasn't. That particular morning the schedule called for the communion service to be early in the worship. Funny thing though, all of a sudden the singing got a lot louder. And even during the next song people were motioning for the ushers to "bring back that juice tray, I was missed". One man poured the cherrios out of his little boy's zip lock bag, and began filling that bag from the disposable cups in the tray. That wouldn't have been so bad, except then he held the bag over head and drank the contents from a hole in one corner.

It was truly amazing what happened during the offering. I believe that Sunday they set a giving record that stands until this day. Although for a moment there it seemed that the whole offertory would turn into a sort of auction when someone shouted "I'll give $100! Which of you hypocrites will match that!" Well, several took that challenge and matched his gift and raised him $10! Finally a couple of ushers had to come down and ask a few of them to leave.

Calm, reverent, loving people who had never visibly disciplined their children suddenly "thumped ears", "poked ribs", and "cuffed" the back of a few heads. Pretty astonishing for a bunch of kids who had never actually heard the word "no" in public before.

People who would have dropped dead if they had heard someone say an audible "Amen" were suddenly shouting "praise the Lord" and "you tell it preacher!" at the wide-eyed minister. Meanwhile both Alfred and Trish had also "partaken" so Trish was "explaining" proper conduct in church in a stage whisper you could hear in the next county. And ol' Alfred got up, counted for a minute, and marched to the "record board" at the back and said "What the heck, there must be a thousand here", and that's what he posted.

It might well be noted that persimmon wine has the marvelous side-effect, it makes you "pucker" so the "praise the Lord" came out something like "PASE TH 'ORD".

It would truly be easy to criticize the Altizers for all this, except the rest of the church knew how many times Alfred had come to them with tears in his eyes, or Trish had almost gotten on her knees, to get some of them to take a few of those duties so everyone could enjoy worship together...and not a soul had helped. And they had to admit that the Altizer's had given it their best, tried their hardest, and that morning things just "got away from them". So not a word was ever said to them about "the morning".

You might have thought that people would have realized how overworked they were, and lined up to help. You might have envisioned people coming up to them and volunteering to "share their load". You might even have reasoned that everyone would have been somewhat embarrassed by their lack of involvement....Naaaaa. One ol' sister sort of summed up the feelings of the whole church when she said "you know, those Altizers are good folks, but they really need to learn how to act better in church".

It is a well traveled belief that one day on the shores of that better place, the Almighty in His Celestial Robes, and with angels sitting on every golden stone, will give some sort of special dispensation to Al and Trish, and folks like them, who just "kept on keepin' on" so that the church would continue to run smoothly and His word would be taught. And personally, I think even the God of heaven is going to laugh about that "persimmon wine incident."

15

Peter, Peter, the Preacher Eater

Peter Hatchet and His wife Stilletto have always prided themselves on being community-minded folks. Peter owns a little store on main street which sells all sorts of cutlery, and His wife, Stilletto, works as a butcher at the local market. Over the years Peter has been approached and persuaded to serve on almost every civic board in town. When 'Ol man Marv Huckelberry wanted to get the local School Superintendent removed from office, they just called for Peter to "run" for the office. And when Jeb Cornrow wanted the local administrator of the hospital "taken down", well, Peter was suddenly seen as the obvious choice for the hospital board. And so went the list of "purgings" and "prunings" Peter had brought about on every board and committee from the Vo-Tech school to the Boy Scouts. However, it is widely known that Peter would never have been as successful had it not been for his wife of 16 years, Stilletto. From her place behind the meat counter at the local market Silletta had "helped things along' by her whispered innuendoes, her smirked comments, and even her bellowed berating of whoever was Peter's latest target. Stilletto would have gladly served on the "shovel committee" at the local feed lot, if it would have advanced the career of her husband, Peter, as he earned the title "Hatch, the Hatchetman".

It should be pointed out that by himself Peter Hatchet was very benign when it comes to serving any worthwhile purpose on any committee or board. He would just sit there and snarl at every suggestion put forth by the object of his wrath. When the time to vote would come, no matter what the issue, he would always begin with "Well, I have some serious reservations about this..." and then try to take the opposite side from everyone else. It's not that he didn't have a fine education, nor was it that Peter wasn't "up" on the latest issues, it was that He just didn't care. It was the "thrill of the chase" and the "blood of conquest" that made his anemic little heart beat faster. After the latest "threat" or "incompetent" was reduced to "yesterday's news", Silletto would sneer and pat Peter on the back and tell him what a "defender of right" he was. However, it was rumored that after they got home, and all the blinds were closed, Stilletto extracted her proper share of the credit. Once, in public, she even referred to Peter as her "poor little mouse".

Peter and Stilletto were members of the local Southwestern Baptist-pure gospel-Pentecostal-Bible Church. And for several years the church had grown and prospered under the preaching of Dr. Bright Light who acted as their evangelist. Contributions were at an all time high. Attendance was soaring as people came to hear the heart-throbbing sermons of Dr. Light.

Finally the little church building couldn't stand the strain without help, so folding chairs were brought in to accommodate the increasing attendance. Speakers were installed so people could sit in their cars and hear the message, and huge screens were placed in the annex and old sanctuary so that everyone who attended could see and hear Dr. Light deliver the Word of the Lord. And everyone was pretty excited about it all....except...

Bro. Packard Studebaker, long time member and constant thorn in the side of the church. Now Bro. Studebaker was now in his late 70's (very late 70's) and he knew that he didn't have enough of his contemporaries left to challenge Dr. Light and all the growth and goodness that was happening at the SBPGPBC (Southwestern Baptist Pure Gospel Pentecostal Bible Church). But that didn't mean that he liked it a little bit. All those new people coming to church often left him having to sit in a chair in the aisle where everyone could see him, which greatly cut into his Sunday "meditation time". It also meant that often someone would realize that a prayer needed offering or a song led, and they would just "call on" Bro. Packard which brought about him being far more involved than he ever wanted to be. So to alleviate himself of all this activity, and get the church "under control" again, Bro. Packard (the man who loved to kiss babies, and tell cute stories to the older kids) enlisted the aid of Bro. and Sis. Peter Hatchet.

The first order of business was to get Peter placed into the highest echelon of the leadership, you know, where the appointments were "for life, or until he got senile and/or died" whichever came first. Then Peter could quietly, but consistently, thwart any and all of Bro. Light's ideas for church expansion.

On several occasions Bro. Light made various attempts to win the favor of Bro. Hatchet, but to no avail. Even when Peter was starting to show signs of working together, Stilletto would carry on her smear campaign between wrappings of Sirloin Tips. It wasn't so much an all out shooting war, it was more like watching someone say "Abracadabra" and pull the carpet from under Bro. Light right where he stood. Finally, by design, each of the other leaders were convinced that "all the problems of this church" were Bro. Light's doing. And who would have ever suspected that the "running low" on toilet paper, or the "White-out shortage" in the office was, in fact, the preacher's fault. But when seen from the perspective of Peter and Stilletto it was a BIG deal!

As if predestined, the time finally came when the 500 members at SBPGPBC had to say good-by to their friend and beloved minister with great regret and tears, while there was a small "party of three" who were having a celebration over his leaving. And having accomplished the goal of vacating the pulpit, the Hatchets made it clear that for Dr. Light, his four children, two dogs, or his pregnant wife Angelica, to stay in that preacher's house, or preach in that pulpit one more Sunday would do "irreparable harm to the church". So with two weeks to find a job, and a month to move from the home their children had come to love, (in fact the only home the two youngest had ever known), the Light's were on the move. All of this happened, of course, after it was made plain that Dr. Light was to be out of his office at the church by Monday "close of business". It was right! It was holy! It was official! And, it was powerful!

Thanks to the reputation of Dr. Light in that church, several of the church members helped support his family until a new pulpit could be secured. And much to the credit of the whole Light Family, they came through it stronger than before. Finally, and mercifully, the Lights were moving to their new home, in a new city, with new people, to a new challenge, with several new scars.

Meanwhile back at SBPGPBC folks were starting to realize that they had a new problem. They had actually given in to Bro. Packard, who was of little actual help to the church, and they had enshrined Peter Hatchet in an office from which they could not kick him. And further, it became evident, that they had also placed Stilletto in a position of considerable power.

As all this was happening, several of the members moved to the "other church" across town, which caused the attendance to drop, the contribution to dwindle, and the morale to plummet. Peter knew that some "scapegoat" had to be found, because 'ol Packard Studebaker wasn't going to back him one inch. So, Peter began the process to put the limelight directly on the Youth Minister. And sure enough, the young man realized what was happening and took a job with a local fast-food chain to escape the whole process.

Now, to everyone concerned it was evident what had happened. Problem was, there wasn't much anyone could do about it. Peter Hatchet had lived up to his reputation again, and two good families had been scarred for life because of his need for power and authority. Did it bother Peter and Stilletto? Not a whit! They just continued to repeat their well-rehearsed lines about how "the church is stronger now", and how all those other folks could "just leave, they weren't very spiritual in the first place".

After this whole sequence had repeated itself four or five times over a period of 25 years, finally someone suggested that all the leadership should put themselves up to be "reconfirmed" as leaders. Well, Bro. Hatchet welcomed the opportunity since he was sure no one would dare oppose him. All the names were put before the whole assembly, and the agreement was that no one with less than 70% approval rate would be allowed to serve. You can imagine the whining and slurping, and "snotting around" that was heard when Bro. Hatchet only got a 2% approval rating. If it hadn't been for his family it might have been closer to 0%. The cry "I was robbed" was heard to echo through the church building late at night as it bounced across the empty pews his pride and arrogance had created. And right behind him was Stilletto, a broken woman...but not too broken that she couldn't remind Peter of his miserable failings from time to time. It is reported that Stilletto Hatchet is the only butcher in history that ever had someone order porkchops and request that "someone else" wrap the meat.

And Bro. Light? Well, he and his family went to another church. They spent money they didn't have because they were forced to move too quickly, so they were indebted more than ever. And they went through all the usual pains of relocation with the kids and kin folk. But the new church welcomed them, sympathized with their feelings, and even reassured them that "they knew perfectly well" what had happened, because it had happened there long ago.

And then they assured them that it would never happen in that church again.

Now, you may be thinking that the preacher took it on the chin, and Bro. Studebaker and Bro. Hatchet won...outright! Not necessarily. You see about three years later Bro. Packard Studebaker passed away. It took the congregation four days to reach a preacher who would agree to come and hold the funeral (the current preacher opted out because of "lack of knowledge of the man"). They finally found 99 year old Bro. Harold Hornblower who was living in a home for the senile in Ohio and paid the air fare for him to come and do the funeral. And the senile ol' brother made numerous remarks about how "God's hatchet" comes to take us all, the audience all snickered (all 12 of them) and later the ones who didn't come to the service cried at having missed the "fun".

But that wasn't the end of it all. You see while that funeral was taking place on earth, somewhere up in the reaches of heaven there was a judgment scene.

And God, who can assume any form He chooses, was randomly appearing to the horrified Bro. Studebaker as every preacher he had ever given "heart scars", and every member whose reputation he had ever undermined. Frankly the look on Studebaker's face was causing the angels to giggle at the justice of it all.

16

The Two Frog Conspiracy

There is a well traveled story that illustrates how things actually work in your average church.

It seems that a man moved from the hustle and bustle of New York City to the quiet Country of the state of Mississippi. This former New Yorker enjoyed the lazy life style, and the wonderful southern drawl of his neighbors. In fact, the only thing that really was upsetting to him, was the fact that he found it hard to get a good night's sleep because of all the frogs that lived in that region. Every night just after sundown it seemed that every frog in America would start to croak, and not being accustomed to such "music" (as the locals called it) he simply could not get a good night's rest. As he lay there awake he was just sure that on his own small pond there must be several hundred, maybe thousands, of frogs all croaking on purpose to keep him awake. Strange thing is he couldn't watch TV, he couldn't listen to his stereo, he couldn't even sit in the kitchen and eat for the infernal croaking of the frogs. After several nights of such ruckus he was even thinking that the frogs were having meetings to see how they could inflict his life with even more suffering.

Although he had purchased the most beautiful home in the entire county, a place envied by all his neighbors, and although he had installed a swimming pool, landscaping, and put lights in every conceivable place on the property still the frogs continued to plague his life.

Finally in desperation he called one of his friends in New York, a man who owned a restaurant that specialized in "Deep South Cooking". He asked his friend if he could use some frog legs. The friend said he could use all he could ship him by air freight. Well, the new southerner was just sure he could ship him 1000 frog legs by the coming week-end, so a deal was struck.

The very next night the man went out to his nearby pond. He was outfitted with a carbide lamp strapped to his head, and a long "giggin' pole" with which to spear the frogs. In all honesty, he figured if he spent an hour a night for a week, he could meet the demand easily. Well, the first night he looked and looked . He looked under the bushes, around the edge of the water, he even peered into the shallows of the pond, with no success. So, he decided that he needed to wade out into the pond and look under some of those lily pads. Actually, all he found was a couple of "sink holes" on the bottom of the pond that caused him to suddenly disappear out of sight of the surface for a few seconds. After several nights of looking, he noticed that the sounds seem to be coming from an old tree some 30 feet from the water's edge. And there in the glow of his carbide light he saw the source of all the noise – two old bull frogs! Now, there were, sure enough, only two of the wrinkled old amphibians, but to listen to them you would have sworn they were a convention of thousands. However, it was just two, and they busied themselves by sitting on a low branch and flicking their long tongues out to snatch every firefly in the area. With all the light that they extinguished with their tongues it is amazing they didn't glow in the dark!

The moral, and parallel to church work, is fairly obvious. In the preceding pages you have read about several types of Bottle Babies that sap the strength from, and basically distract the intent of whole congregations of God's people.

They look harmless enough, and they make all the sounds that someone of their makeup should make, but the effect is to capture the attention of the leadership of most groups. Like those two old frogs they make it their business to make such "spiritual sounding noise" that no one else can even start to think about what God would have the church do, nor raise their voice loud enough to he heard over the din.

Now you might wonder how just a very few BB's can raise such a ruckus as to distract a whole church. Actually it is their heart-born cry that makes it possible. These BB's are well equipped, but spiritually deficient, enough to have their voice heard over every God glorifying effort the church might put forth. They use such croaks as "you know there are a lot of people...", or

"well I know several people who agree with me on this...", or the loudest croak of all, "No one believes.....". Some develop a sort of specialized croak based on their inflated estimation of their charity it goes something like this, "Well, I give a lot of money and...". Or maybe the croak is based on years of doing absolutely nothing but pew sit, that sound is," Well, you know I am a charter member of this church!" One of these frog type BB's was heard to say in a sugary sweet voice "preachers may come and preachers may go, but I'm still here."

Like their amphibious counterparts, these BB's usually have only two functions. First, they spread their warts to other unsuspecting members of the church. Do not be deceived there will always be some younger member who will find a reason to look up to this Bottle Baby frog. And after a while, they will start to use the same lingo, and possess the same "I just found a piece of chewing gum in the chicken coop" look on their face when they are around the working members of the church. These croakers come in very small numbers, but they are deft at converting weaker members to their numbers, and by so doing they can stand back and let the new recruits do the croaking for them.

Also be assured that "doing nothing" is the favorite pastime of the croaking BB's.

You couldn't drive one of them to teach a Bible class, or lead a program, or approach someone for the purpose of evangelism with a ten foot giggin' pole.

The second function of this sort of BB is that they make it their business to rid the church of any and all light that might happen to stray into the assembly.

With tongues longer and sharper than any amphibian we know of, they can find something wrong with any new program, gripe, whine and complain about any new thing that might bring a measure of joy and forward motion to the church. When it comes to singing, they don't like "those ol' camp songs", forgetting that Rock of Ages was probably new at some point in time.

When it comes to the meeting house, the same old pews with the same old carpet will do just fine, because after all "my ol' granddaddy helped smooth out the concrete in this building while grandma helped lay the bricks". Never mind that the concrete, like their reasoning, had cracked after years of use.

If you mentioned missions they would croak about how "missionaries are just getting rich with all the money we're sending them". But if you spoke of a program for the local church, then they would sit up tall and proud and speak of how they "were involved in foreign missions". By interpretation that means "I send $25 dollars every three months to Mongolia so I can feel justified in doing absolutely nothing at home". And can't you just imagine how that Mongolian missionary feels, while living in a country where almost none of the finer things of our country even exist, once a month he receives the "coke money" from some American with a note about how he "should be careful not to spend it in one place, nor frivolously." Sort of brings a warm glow to your heart to just read about it doesn't it?

And of course, if the local church should decide on some project that would benefit the community at home the BB frog will start to croak about how "People will just take advantage of the church" and "you know those folks could do better if they really wanted to!"

Bring up a controversial topic at church, no matter if it is divorce and re-marriage, giving, the Holy Spirit, the Inerrancy of the Bible, How many angels can dance on the head of a pin, or any other "heavy theological issue" and the BB will be there to regurgitate every worn out witticism they have ever heard from a preacher in their past. But rest assured you will never have to get into a sure-enough Bible discussion with a BB. You can't argue using something of which you have no knowledge.

Things that bring smiles, joy, love, warm feelings, spiritual awakenings, and close brotherly love are matters that drive Bottle Babies crazy! And if they have never been tried before – making them new to the BB – then as they say "everybody is against the whole thing". The real problem is BB's are, by nature, against anything that they don't know anything about. And that takes in a whole lot of territory.

Once a "discussion" (church speak for "fight") broke out over the issue of "is it all right for a person to have a teaspoon of wine each day for medical purposes?" One BB objected strenuously because "it would surely lead them to drunkenness, and God condemns all use of wine." When it was pointed out that Jesus actually turned water into wine on one occasion, the BB replied, "Yes, and I've wondered about Him ever since."

In leadership circles, these croaking BB's can be the death knell to any church. Once when a BB leader was trying to promote killing the outreach ministry of his church on financial grounds, someone pointed out that the Bible was implicit about how we should try to reach out to the lost. The BB retorted with "The Bible doesn't matter in here, this is a business meeting!"

Having pointed out all these things, **let it be known that there is real hope.**

You see all of the BB's, in the leadership and out, men and women, members with tenure and without, all put together comprise less than 10% of any church. They just sound like a majority. And they want to sound like a majority. But "everyone believes" really means "I think, and my husband better agree with me". And "there's a lot of people upset" is just church speak for "This is going to mess with my Sunday afternoon football game".

And don't forget the venerated, "There are some dangerous things going on here!", which decodes into "if you keep that up I might have to get involved and I really don't have any intention of doing so."

So, what shall we do about the "Two Frog Conspiracy" of the BB's of the church? My option is, "don't give them the time of day." Instead, when they start to whine, blubber, carp, croak, and slobber about some small minded topic, listen for a second, and then ask "What was the topic in the last class you taught?" And then when they say they have never taught ask "well, what do you intend to teach next quarter in your class?" When they say they have no talent for teaching and therefore don't intend to teach, look them dead in the eye and ask "then if you don't teach, and don't intend to teach, which committees to do you serve on?" And when they say they don't do that either, then ask "tell me why you think I should listen to you on this subject?"

That is the real Achilles heel of the BB. Immature, non-active, negative pew sitter should not be allowed to foist their carping opinion on anyone, much less a leader in the church. Ministers should be diligently protected from such people. Board members, committee chairs, and Elders and deacons should be shielded from them like the President is shielded by the Secret Service. Why? Because if they steal the spiritual zeal of your leaders, they have controlled the church. And no church (regardless of its problems) deserves that.

Actually a friend of mine had a great idea that I hope will one day catch on. His idea was that all of the churches in a given vicinity should send all their Bottle Babies to a congregation organized and designed just for them. Take that 10% from ten churches you have a whole church of Bottle Babies. Think of it, we could call it the "First Nursery Church" and of course over time there would have to be a North Side and a South Side congregation.

Barring that, we just have to love them, put up with them, and try to grow in spite of them. But never let the mainstream, forward moving body of the church ever allow the Bottle Babies to keep them from moving forward toward heaven. Making them mad is OK, even an occasional verbal spanking might be in order. But in no instance should they be allowed to "drive the car"; babies don't do those sort of things, especially the slurping types.

Just think about those two old frogs making all that racket and smile knowingly.

www.ingramcontent.com/pod-product-compliance
Ingram Content Group UK Ltd.
Pitfield, Milton Keynes, MK11 3LW, UK
UKHW020139250726
13967UKWH00002B/750